S0-BMS-374

Walking Hand in Hand
with Cameron,
Together We Can!

Walking Hand in Hand with Cameron, Together We Can!

One Family's Journey with Cerebral Palsy

Becki Enck, MPH

Macquarie
Regional Library

iUniverse, Inc.
New York Bloomington Shanghai

Walking Hand in Hand with Cameron, Together We Can!
One Family's Journey with Cerebral Palsy

Copyright © 2008 by Becki Enck

All rights reserved. No part of this book may be used or reproduced by any means, graphic, electronic, or mechanical, including photocopying, recording, taping or by any information storage retrieval system without the written permission of the publisher except in the case of brief quotations embodied in critical articles and reviews.

iUniverse books may be ordered through booksellers or by contacting:

iUniverse
1663 Liberty Drive
Bloomington, IN 47403
www.iuniverse.com
1-800-Authors (1-800-288-4677)

Because of the dynamic nature of the Internet, any Web addresses or links contained in this book may have changed since publication and may no longer be valid.

The views expressed in this work are solely those of the author and do not necessarily reflect the views of the publisher, and the publisher hereby disclaims any responsibility for them.

ISBN: 978-0-595-49005-9 (pbk)
ISBN: 978-0-595-60926-0 (ebk)

Printed in the United States of America

Abby and Cameron,

You inspire me to be everything that I can be!

Love,
Mommy

In Loving Memory of:
My big brother Jerry
My Dad
My Gram BoBo

Contents

Foreword by Dr. Henry Mangurten, MD

This is the story of a child ... a mother ... a family who endured a painful and unexpected event which threatened to plunge them into a future of doom and gloom. But the mother, Becki Enck, with sheer resolve, determination and an unbreakable spirit, literally converted the setback into an opportunity and a future of HOPE for her child.

Enck, refusing to accept that her young infant, Cameron, was destined for a future of severe disability and total dependence, literally turned things around. After a calloused and uncaring pediatric neurology fellow demeaned Enck and her husband, Tim, for allowing Cameron (Cam) to be placed on a ventilator, the infant defied the prognosis and eventually tolerated weaning off the ventilator. His recovery served as a catalyst for his mother's subsequent health care choices. When a physician in their initial pediatric practice was too casual in managing Cam during an acute illness, she changed to another pediatric practice. When Cam developed seizures at seven weeks age, the new pediatricians recommended a pediatric neurologist whose philosophy of hope and "never say die" mirrored Enck's philosophy. In fact, his admonition of "the day that we say Cam will never do something, he never will!" has served as her life-defining credo. Ironically this neurologist delivered some bad news during this first evaluation of Cam. But his honest approach was tempered with compassion, empathy, patience and above all, HOPE.

Cameron's story is actually his mother's story. The book chronicles her energetic, painstaking efforts to seek out the best medical care, therapies and educational opportunities for her young son. Refusing to be locked in by conventional expectations for a child with a diagnosis of "cerebral palsy," she breaks thru barrier after barrier until she finds the best fit for Cam. One especially poignant episode involves a group of mothers with children in Cam's play group. These women view Cam as a negative influence for their own "normal" children. Enck, deeply hurt, sheds them and moves on, eventually finding more worldly, intelligent and tolerant friends. Similarly when speech therapists show up late or not at all for home sessions, she makes a change. When an orthopedic surgeon refuses to listen to Enck, ignoring her concerns and perceptions regarding Cam's problems, she finds a more family-centered orthopedist. When the school district in which they live falls short in promising resources which Cam will require, Enck initiates a process which results in the family moving to a different school district. Every decision she makes is intended to maximize opportunities for Cam and his older sister. Enck is the ultimate ... the MODEL ... advocate for her children!

The results are dramatic! Cam demonstrates achievements in his first five years of life which surpass even his mother's expectations. This is a testimonial to the human spirit, to an individual mother's fortitude and refusal to give up on any challenge that threatens her child's future.

This is must reading for professionals who manage infants and children at risk for lifelong disability. It serves as a critical reminder of the need to include empathy and proper choice of words and body language when sharing potentially devastating news with parents. But this book is more than a guide for health care and educational professionals. It also serves as a roadmap for parents of at-risk children, with a message of never giving up until all searches for the best resources are exhausted. To do less is an opportunity lost; to follow Becki Enck's lead is a potential door-opener for every child at risk for lifelong disability!

Henry Mangurten, M.D.
Chairman, Department of Pediatrics
Advocate Lutheran General Children's Hospital

Foreword by Julie Samuelson, BSN, MSN

A classic research study by Olshansky (1962) discovered the phenomenon termed 'chronic sorrow' which was often seen as a result of the many and significant physical and emotional demands of parenting a disabled child as they experienced delays in the achievement of some, or many, physical and developmental milestones.

Becki Enck's story of her family's journey though the first four and one half years of her son's life—a little blonde boy, who climbs on everything, sings the Jeopardy song and infects you with his contagious smile ... reframes that previous phenomenon to one of **chronic hope**! Becki teaches us the surprisingly simple, yet profound lesson of the impact our words can, **and do have** on those we serve—patients and family who are first and foremost, sons, mothers, sisters and DaDas—families who will experience limitations and regression if only labeled as a diagnosis, but have potential to exceed all expectations if we enable them to do so.

The simplicity in the lessons Becki shares is that it's really all a matter of respect—honoring the patient as a unique, individual of worth—regardless of a real/potential diagnosis, valuing the family as the people who know the patient better than anyone, and actively listening with our hearts as well as our minds. All patients and families deserve the opportunity to experience a patient-centered experience—the best that healthcare has to offer. I thank Becki for teaching us what that can look like through the examples of Dr. Shah and others. We will forever be in her debt.

As Christopher Reeves shared, "By choosing hope, everything is possible!"

Julie J. Samuelson, RN, MSN
Sr. Vice President
The Patient-Centered Care Institute

Foreword by Andi Andree, B.S.Ed., M.S.Ed.

To say that I am honored to write a foreword for Becki's book would be an understatement. Becki's drive, determination and hard work to educate the medical field, parents of children with special needs, current and future educators and anyone else that is open to understanding how important it is to allow all children to reach their potential is to be admired.

Two years ago my local paper featured an article that grabbed my attention; it was about Becki's story. What struck me was the very important message that Becki was giving. Her message was to never prejudge a child's potential. As a special educator for over 30 years I live by this motto. As a part time instructor at Northern Illinois University I strive to deliver this message to my class of future educators. I immediately wrote Becki an e-mail and asked her if she would be interested in speaking to my NIU class. Becki had not had this type of audience at the time but was very excited about the opportunity. Since that time she has spoken to many of my classes and has made a permanent and positive impact on all of my students. I have asked my students to write a reaction paper after her talk and the following are a few quotes from these future teachers:

> "I have learned as a parent as well as a teacher one should never set limitations for children."
> "Everyone involved with a child needs to be acknowledged as part of the team and stay optimistic in their beliefs about what the individual can do."
> "Differences make people BEAUTIFUL."

When Becki was going to speak to my class for the first time I wanted to get her a thank you gift for her time. I went to my local Ben Franklin store and looked around for a gift. It was difficult, as I did not know her at the time. I then saw a gift that had the word "Hope" on it and it felt right. I wondered if it was appropriate and how Becki would react. On that night I gave Becki the gift and then she told me she had a gift for me. I was surprised that she would bring me a gift when she was the one doing me a favor. I then opened my box and inside was a silver stone with the word "Hope" on it. We now have a very special connection and I am grateful that Becki has become a friend to me.

I realize that Cam is a very young child at the time of this writing. He, along with Becki, Tim and Abby will have many joyous moments with Cam but they will also have some struggles. The biggest struggles will not be with Cam himself; they will be when others do not see him for who he is. It will take a lot of patience on all of their parts as they strive to educate others to what seems like common sense to them. I have fought this battle for many years, not as a parent, but as an educator and advocate for individuals with special needs. Sometimes, we that live in this special world of understanding need to remember that others do not live in this same world. On the first night of my classes at NIU I ask my students to write down any questions they have for me. One question made me think and realize some philosophies that I live by and hope to teach to others. The question was, "How have you been able to teach students with special needs for so long? I heard that the burn out rate was very high." My answer to this student was that I feel we are all the same. I am no better than anyone and no one is better than me. Do I admire others for accomplishments they may have made? Absolutely. Do I feel they are better than me? Absolutely not. I give the example that while teaching at Sycamore High School I regard our custodians with utmost respect. I do the same with our superintendent. I do not feel above the custodians or below the superintendent. I know and respect all these individuals for the contributions they are giving to our young students. This translates into how I feel about my students, or anyone for that matter, that has a disability. Why would I ever feel better than them? I cannot understand why others may feel that way. Maybe it is a way of protecting themselves from people they have not had the pleasure of knowing and feeling apprehensive about the unknown.

The other philosophy is that we all have a unique potential. One of my student's potential is to have someone who they can truly call a friend. Another student's goal is to be gainfully employed. Interesting how these goals do not sound much different than most people. That is because we are all more the same than we are different.

At the high school I want to teach my students to love and respect themselves. Each one has a unique talent and interest. Most lack the confidence or have the knowledge on how to reach that potential. Too many times they have been told about their weaknesses. Okay, let's realize our weaknesses, make adaptations to compensate for them and zero in on our strengths. Ryan, a student in my class, can skateboard better than I ever will. Should I feel inadequate that I do not have this skill? Absolutely not. Should he zero in on the fact that he has the motor ability to do this well? Absolutely. Ryan's learning disability leaves him struggling in academics. If he gains the confidence and drive that it will take for him to succeed his many strengths can take him far. Ross has been diagnosed with autism. He struggles socially and academically as a result. The Early Intervention he received, paired with his best advocate, his mother, and her relentless drive for Ross to reach his potential has allowed him to surpass many milestones that many said would never happen. Ross drives himself to school each day. His honesty has gained the love of the student body as he was voted Homecoming King this past year. Why do I mention these stories? They can be applied to each individual. People with a disability are in a minority. So are certain ethnic groups and religions. If you live long enough either you are someone you love will join this minority. It is the only minority that you can join at any moment. I will not be a member of a different ethnic group tomorrow but I could be disabled.

It just makes sense. We are all the same. Feel grateful that you can read this. If someone is reading it to you be grateful that you can hear the words. If someone's disability does not allow him or her to read or hear this are they less of a person? Absolutely not. Get to know all people. Do not hide behind what is unknown to you by not accepting people with disabilities. We are all the same.

Learn from Becki, Tim, Abby and Cam. Be grateful for Dr. Shah. Thank you for sharing your story Becki.

Andi Andree, B.S.Ed., M.S.Ed.
Sycamore High School, Vocational Instructor
Northern Illinois University, Instructor

Acknowledgments

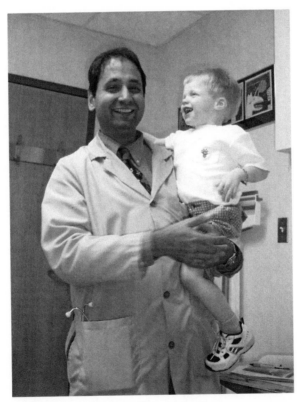

Cameron with Dr. Nishant Shah, Director of Pediatric Neurology at Advocate
Lutheran General Hospital in Park Ridge, Illinois

Dr. Nishant Shah, you are the most inspiring gentleman we have ever met. You
have the ability to provide your patients and their families with hope when
other medical professionals would not. When you told us "The day you say
Cameron will never do something, he never will" you provided us with the

life philosophy that we needed to make sure that we would be able to help Cameron be all that he can be! You are such an important person to our family. I know when we have told you how much of an impact you have had on Cameron's life you tell us that we give you too much credit—but the truth is we could never give you enough credit Dr. Shah. As our thanks to you we promise to always provide Cameron with every opportunity that he needs to be all that he can be!

Abby and Cam with Me-Mom (my Mom)

Mom, you are certainly the most loving and caring woman I know! You have taught me through example what it means to never give up and to give 100% of yourself to someone you love. You amazed me with all of the strength, determination and unconditional love you demonstrated as you took care of Dad through his long and difficult battle with Zoellinger-Ellison Syndrome (a rare pancreatic disease). You played many roles those last few years of his life, including being his caregiver as well as his advocate. You made sure that he received the best medical care available and that he was always treated with dignity and respect. It was not until I was faced with caring for Cameron during that first year that I gained some understanding of what your life was like the last five years that Dad was with us. Thank you so much for taking such amazing care of Dad and for teaching me through example how to take care of Cameron. I admire and love you so much Mom!

Introduction

Does it Take a Village to Raise a Child?

I remember hearing Hilary Clinton on many occasions state that it takes a village to raise a child, an ancient African proverb. I also remember thinking what does Hilary Clinton mean by that? I thought why would it take an entire village to raise a child? Surely it could not be that all encompassing. It was not until our second child, Cameron, was born that I truly grasped the meaning of this statement. Going from one child to two children did not change my mind about the validity of this proverb. However, adding a child with special needs did. It taught me how important of a role a village can play and does play in the raising of our children, Abby and Cameron.

Our daughter, Abby, was only nineteen months old when she became the proud big sister to Cameron. She was fascinated by him from the moment she first laid her eyes on him. Imagine her surprise and ours when she took a jump back from the isolette he was laying in when he started to yawn and stretch his arms. Until that moment I truly think she thought he was just a beautiful baby doll that looked so similar to her. But when he started to move she was just amazed! I will forever have that moment etched in my mind—the moment that I became a mom to two children and a moment that was so typical for other families with two children. This would be one of those rare typical two children moments for Tim and me because our world would forever change when Cameron was just six days old. We would become a very different family of four than any of our other friends and family members.

Despite concerns over Cameron's lethargy, absentee cry and disinterest in feeding, Cameron and I were discharged from the hospital two days after he was born. He slept through the night the first night home and he never woke up for any of his feedings. I had to keep waking him. And we had still not heard him cry. I called the pediatrician to express my concerns but was told that unlike his premature sister, Cameron was a full-term baby and full-term babies are not nearly as colicky as preemies are. He also told us to be thankful to be getting a full night's sleep already since most new parents are so sleep deprived.

Unfortunately, my suspicions that something was wrong with Cameron were correct. At six days of age, Cameron cried the entire night and nothing I did could soothe him. By morning he had developed a rectal temperature of 101.6 F. Soon we would learn how truly serious a fever is in a newborn. After multiple spinal taps, being placed on a ventilator and numerous medical complications, Cameron was diagnosed with suspected meningitis. He received the antibiotic regimen for meningitis and at one month of age was discharged home as a normal, healthy newborn. However, we would soon learn that this was not the case; he was not a healthy newborn.

At seven weeks of age, Cameron displayed seizure-like activity and due to a switch in pediatricians he was admitted to another hospital for testing. It was that day our lives would forever change. It was that day that would later make us realize that we needed a village to help us to raise our children. At seven weeks of age an MRI showed that Cameron had suffered extensive brain damage and brain atrophy. The damage was consistent with a cerebral palsy diagnosis, a diagnosis that would later be confirmed at one year of age.

Unbeknownst to us, our village expanded that day to include Dr. Nishant Shah, the Director of Pediatric Neurology at Advocate Lutheran General Hospital in Park Ridge, Illinois. Dr. Shah delivered the news of Cameron's MRI results to us. He spent over two hours with us that evening. He allowed us time to cry, to ask the same questions over and over and to trust that he would provide all of the support we would need to help Cameron. That night Dr. Shah defined the "rules" of our village. As we questioned him about whether Cameron would ever learn to walk, talk or play with toys, Dr. Shah told us "The day you say Cameron will never do something, he never will!" He not only educated us about the importance of providing Cameron with Early Intervention therapies but he also contacted Early Intervention for us to begin the process of helping Cameron to become everything that he can be.

When Cameron was discharged from the hospital we brought him home and did not share the results of his MRI with anyone. We decided to be our own village. After all, we did not need a village to raise our children, we could do it alone. And we believed that if we did not tell anyone about Cameron's brain damage then maybe it really would not be true. We were not ready to hear others thoughts and opinions, let alone anyone's inability to accept the fact that our child had special needs. Within three weeks we learned how much we needed support. One day I broke down crying to my mom and shared what we had learned. She could not have been more supportive and has continued to be our main support person. She became the second member of our village. A lifetime member that we knew would provide us with words of support, a shoulder to lean on, and arms to carry us as we began our journey into special-needs parenting and continue along its' pathway.

People often ask me how I survived that first year. I honestly tell them that I am not sure if I would say I survived but rather I would say I existed. I cried every single day, especially at night after Tim, Abby and Cameron went to bed. I actually sobbed. I cried thinking about all of the painful procedures Cam had to endure at one week of age. I cried thinking about the many times that I had to leave Abby with my mom so that I could care for Cameron in the hospital. I cried because I believed and still do believe that if that pediatrician would have listened to my concerns after Cam was born and had run some blood tests then Cam would have received antibiotics sooner and would not have suffered extensive brain damage. And I cried because more than anything I loved my son with all of my heart and the uncertainty of his future felt unbearable. I did not only cry at night, sometimes I cried in the day too. I cried often during Cameron's therapy sessions. I found support from Cameron's therapists and I found that they were excellent listeners. It was safe to be open and honest with them and I welcomed the opportunity to not have to put on a smile and pretend to be okay when some days I was not. And I had the good fortune to meet Angela, the parent liaison for our Early Intervention office who provided support as a fellow parent of a child with special needs. She was a source of support and strength for me. Angela was there to listen and let me cry when Cameron would plateau in therapy and she was there to celebrate each and every achievement of Cameron's regardless of its' magnitude. And so entered many more members of our village.

Throughout that first year, Cameron had many other medical complications and by the end of the first year he was also seeing a pediatric pulmonologist, pediatric ear, nose and throat specialist, pediatric orthopedist and pediatric allergist. And again, I found that our village expanded more, to include many different medical professionals.

Did we allow anyone to enter our village? Yes, we did. However, there were some members whose membership was revoked. On a few occasions we encountered medical professionals who wanted to place limitations on Cameron and we could not allow that. We could not say that Cameron would never do something because then he would not. It was during those times, when the philosophy Dr. Shah shared with us became key to our ability to get up each day and face the day with a positive attitude and a sense of hope. We also encountered some "friends" who were also not very accepting of differences and so we made the choice to walk away from those friendships, a decision that we know was the right decision for our family.

When we started our journey into special needs parenting and I began to realize that it would take a village to help raise not only our children but our family, I had a preconceived idea about who would be members of our village. I automatically assumed that it would include each family member, all of our friends and also medical professionals. I did not realize that my preconceived idea of our village would not resemble our actual village. Yes, our village does include family members, friends and medical professionals. However, it is not every family member. In fact, some of our immediate family members never even attempted to join our village. We do have friends in our village, friends who are very diverse, some who have a child with special needs and some who do not. However, not all of original friends are members. And finally, I never would have imagined the level of support and involvement the members of Cameron's medical team would play in our lives. The unending support we receive as a family in addition to the medical support that Cameron receives is truly astonishing.

And so yes, I have concluded that it does take a village to raise a child, particularly a child with special needs. And the composition of members in the village might be very different than expected. I am so thankful to each and every member of our village, because of each of them not only is Cameron going to become everything that he can be, but so are we, his mom, his dad and his very loved big sister Abby!

And so "Walking Hand in Hand with Cameron, Together We Can" is not only our family's journey with cerebral palsy, but also our family's discovery of our village!

What qualifies me to write this book?

In addition to being Cameron's mom, I hold a Master's Degree of Public Health with an emphasis in Health Promotion and Health Education from Northern Illinois University in DeKalb, Illinois. I am also an active member of Cam's team, a team of medical specialists, therapists and school professionals who are all committed to helping Cameron to become everything that he can be!

Who is this book written for?

This book is for parents of children with special needs so that they will know that the feelings they are feeling upon learning of their child's special needs and throughout their journey are normal and that they are not alone in feeling what they feel. The hardest part of our journey at the start was to express our true feelings because we feared that others would criticize us for feeling scared, angry, helpless and all of the other feelings we felt. Yes, we were and still are so thankful that Cameron survived the meningitis and yes, we realize that there are many parents that are not as fortunate as we are, but that does not mean that there is something wrong with us for feeling the feelings we felt. We have learned that feelings are not right or wrong, they are what they are and what we choose to do with them is what is important. We chose to feel and share the feelings we felt so we could move forward with our lives and truly enjoy each and every moment with Abby and Cameron.

This book is also for medical professionals so that they will understand how important it is to remember to treat each of their patients with care and compassion. Words that are spoken will be forever remembered and actions are observed. Remember as you work with your patients that they are also someone's son, daughter, mother, father, brother, sister and/or friend. And please, remember as you are delivering a diagnosis that the manner in which you speak to a patient or patient's family can impact that patient's future outcome.

This book is also for educators. You will have the ability to become an important part of a child and a family's life each time you accept a new student into your classroom. Please strive each and every day to help our children to become everything they can be!

Finally, this book is intended to educate each and every person who reads it to never place limitations on anyone, after all "The day you say someone will never do something, they never will!"

Our Family

This is a story about our son Cameron. We have told his story so often to each other and those who ask, but today we want to share his story with the world. As you read his story, you will see that no matter what medical challenges you face in your life or your child's life, you always need to have hope. You will also understand the power of unconditional love as you see what an amazing part Cameron's big sister, Abby, has played in his life.

Tim and I have known each other for ten years and have been married for nine years. We have had so many wonderful moments together and we have weathered some very difficult moments together as well. We were married in Maui and our wedding day was a dream come true day. When we said our vows we said them with 100% commitment. I can remember vowing to stay together for richer or for poorer, in sickness and in health and in good times and in bad. To be honest we never imagined that we would really have some bad times. We loved one another and we had a bright and happy future to look forward to. We knew that we would experience some of life's sad moments like every other couple but never did we imagine what was to come.

We are blessed to have two children, Abby who is now six-years-old and Cameron who is four-and-a-half-years-old. Both of our children are heroes in our eyes—they have taught us what it means to work very hard for what you want, what it means to love someone unconditionally and above all that you always have to have hope.

Abby was born prematurely at thirty-four weeks, after my water broke at twenty-nine weeks gestation. I had experienced PROM (premature rupture of membranes), which is defined as a leakage of amniotic fluid prior to the onset of labor. Due to the risk of infection and serious harm to a fetus, medical monitoring is required and therefore I was on hospital bed rest for thirty-seven days prior to Abby's arrival. From the start, Abby was eager to enter the world and to amaze us every step of the way. Although she was placed on CPAP (continuous positive airway pressure used to keep the airway open) after birth, she only remained in the Neonatal Intensive Care Unit (NICU) for eleven days and came home on an apnea monitor. She had no additional health issues despite her prematurity. She was our artistic child who at only nine months of age would sit and color for an hour at a time. She started to talk at about the same time, and quickly amazed us with her growing vocabulary and communication skills. It seemed like she was talking in sentences in no time. She was also fiercely independent—dressing herself all on her own by eighteen months of age and constantly telling us "I do it!" when encountering any new situation. She very rarely let us help her. I guess that is why we knew she would be a great big sister.

Cameron was born full-term, thirty-seven weeks gestation, and was completely opposite of his sister from the start. Whereas Abby was colicky, Cameron was a very quiet, content baby. In fact he did not even cry when he was delivered and slept through the night his first night home from the hospital. Although we questioned his pediatrician about his lack of crying and waking, we were assured that he was just a lazy baby unlike his high strung premature big sister. Unfortunately, we would learn that his disposition was not truly that content, but rather he was sick.

Our first family photo of the 4 of us—Cam was one day old

And He Cried ...

When Cameron was six days old he did begin to cry. He cried through the night and although I was able to soothe him for short periods of time, for the most part we were both awake the entire evening. By morning Cameron developed a rectal temperature of 101.6 F and a call to the pediatrician resulted in a trip to the ER. Upon arriving at the ER we learned that a fever in a neonate is quite dangerous and can be indicative of a serious infection, meningitis. We were told that they would perform a spinal tap on Cameron to see if he did indeed have meningitis and he would be admitted to the hospital while we awaited the tap results. Several unsuccessful spinal taps later, Cameron was started on the antibiotic treatment for meningitis. By the next evening Cameron's fever was diminishing and he was perking up. So I sent Tim home to spend time with Abby while I stayed with Cameron. Little did I know what a mistake I had made sending Tim home.

About two hours after Tim left, I was holding Cameron when he began to experience rapid eye blinking. His breathing became labored. I called the nurse who in turn paged the on-call pediatrician. By the time the pediatrician arrived, Cameron's eye blinking had worsened and his breathing grew even more labored. The doctor immediately informed me that Cameron was in serious condition; he was experiencing a seizure and was in need of assistance. She also decided that Cameron was too ill to remain at their hospital and she would be arranging for an emergency transport to a Chicago-area hospital. Then she asked for my permission to have Cameron placed on a ventilator and of course I said yes immediately. One of the nurses called the hospital chaplain and he came up to be by my side. He asked where my husband was and together we called him to return to the hospital immediately. That was the worst call I have ever had to make in my life. I was so scared that Tim would get in an accident driving forty-five minutes back to the hospital. Tim called my mom who lived on our street and within a minute she arrived to stay with Abby so he could leave. The chaplain was told the situation was worsening and so he asked me what our religious beliefs were and recommended having Cameron baptized prior to the transport. He called and arranged for a Catholic priest to come right over. Then the chaplain asked if we had anyone else to join me at the hospital while we waited for Tim to arrive. Immediately I thought of my Aunt Sandy who lived only minutes away. When I called her she answered immediately. I do not remember exactly what I told her but she arrived within ten minutes to help. She was my source of strength while I watched as my little boy lay listless on his hospital bed—many nurses and doctors surrounded him and worked feverishly to get him ventilated and stabilized. As soon as the ventilator was placed, the pediatrician came out to talk to me and my aunt. She informed us that Cameron was in critical condition and that a transport was being arranged. The problem was that the weather was not going to permit a helicopter transport so a ground transport team was being sent from a Chicago-area hospital to pick Cameron up and take him to the hospital. I remember asking the doctor if I could accompany Cam during the transport and she said she was pretty sure that they would allow me to ride along. After the team arrived and assessed Cameron they came out to tell us what would happen. Tim arrived just in time. The transport team said that we would be leaving in a few minutes regardless of whether or not the priest arrived. Luckily, the priest arrived just as they were getting ready to place Cameron in the transport unit and quickly baptized Cameron with Tim, my aunt, and a few nurses surrounding him. We all held hands and prayed that he would survive the transport. And then we were off. I can remember sitting in the front seat of the ambulance and Tim standing by the window. We were holding hands and crying while the team was getting Cameron ready in the back of the ambulance for the transport. Once he was ready we were off. I remember watching Tim wave good-bye and wondering if we would ever be a family of four again.

Although the ambulance traveled as quickly as possible to the hospital, it was a Friday night and traffic entering the city of Chicago was heavy and moving quite slow. Even though the sirens were blasting it really did not help much with the traffic jam. By the time we arrived at the hospital Tim was also entering the ER entrance. So we walked behind the team as they pushed Cameron up to the NICU (Neonatal Intensive Care Unit). We were told that Cameron would be admitted to the NICU even though technically he should have gone to the PICU (Pediatric Intensive Care Unit) since he was a neonate who had been discharged to home. Due to the seriousness of his condition, the transporting physician received permission for a NICU admission. When Cameron was removed from the incubator unit and placed in the unit in the NICU he was listless. He just lay completely still. The ventilator was helping him to breathe and he was allowing it. He was not making any attempts of his own. I remember sitting with Tim about ten feet away and just watching as the NICU team assessed Cameron's condition and then came over to tell us what was happening. Basically, Cameron had experienced a seizure and due to his inability to properly breathe he was placed on the ventilator. He also was not regulating his body temperature so a warming blanket was placed under him and lights were placed above him. We were told he was in critical condition. Due to the seriousness of his condition they were starting an IV in his head and they were replacing his IV in his arm. Although we were not allowed to stay at his bedside throughout the evening, we were allowed to stay on the floor in a parent room. I remember one of the staff members showing us to the room, giving us blankets, towels and instructions on how to use the phone so we could update our families on what was happening. We chose to make only two phone calls; one to my mom who was staying at our house with Abby and one to Tim's parents. And we asked them to pass along the information to other family members and friends. I remember making sure to tell my mom to call and check on my Aunt Sandy to make sure she was home safely.

Throughout the evening we took turns checking in with Cameron's nurse to make sure he was okay. He remained in critical but stable condition. We were also told that first thing in the morning the attending neurologist would be up to see Cameron and several tests would be ordered. Since we would not be allowed in the NICU during morning rounds, Tim and I both decided to grab a shower in preparation for a long day at the hospital. We also grabbed breakfast from the vending machines and waited outside the NICU for the physicians to complete their rounds. After rounds, we entered the NICU and were able to grab two chairs and sit by Cameron. He was on the ventilator, had an IV in his head and several other pieces of equipment attached to him. He looked so vulnerable and so little and yet he was so still that he looked at peace.

Around 10 am or so the neurologist came to see Cameron. We were under the assumption that this was the attending neurologist, but in fact we would learn much later that this was a fellow. He asked us a question or two about my pregnancy and Cameron's delivery and then proceeded to examine Cameron. He was unable to bend Cameron's arms or legs and it was the first time that Tim and I realized that Cameron was not able to move his limbs. He then told us something that no parent should ever hear, he said "Your son should not have been placed on life support—if he does survive he will have no functionality—he is paralyzed and showing no signs of any brain functioning based on my assessment." With that he said good-bye and that he would see us the next day. And he left. He did not ask us if we had any questions, he did not offer his condolences or anything.

After the neurologist left, I remember looking at Tim and then going over and trying to hold Cameron's hand. I guess I thought that Cameron was not responding to the doctor because he did not know him. I knew that he would wrap his hand around my finger as he had after birth. It was then that I realized that Cameron was not squeezing my finger back. He just laid still. And yet he was not asleep. And I started to feel an overwhelming sense of sadness. I felt like I could barely breathe, no matter how hard I tried. I told Tim that I needed him to take me home for a little while because I needed to hold Abby in my arms and for one more moment feel like a family. So we told the nurse we were leaving. She tried to talk us into staying. She had overheard the entire conversation of the neurologist which we would later learn. We did leave. It took us almost two hours to get home.

When we arrived home my mom and Abby were sitting on the couch in the family room and we all hugged. Then Tim took Abby upstairs and I sat down by my mom and I remember saying "How am I going to go on without my Cameron. We have only had him in our lives for one week but already I love him so much and I can't live without him. How am I going to do this?" My mom just held me and told me that I would find the strength to do what I had to do. We decided to have dinner and then pack some of our things to return to the hospital. When we sat down to eat the phone rang and it was the hospital. I started to cry. I thought for sure they were calling to tell us our son had passed away. I just sat shaking as my husband talked. When he hung up the phone he told me that was one of the attending physicians who was calling because the nurse had told him what had happened earlier with the neurologist and he wanted us to return to the hospital. He told Tim that Cameron was already showing signs of improvement. So we quickly gathered our belongings, kissed Abby good-bye and made the drive to the hospital.

When we entered the NICU the attending doctor was waiting at Cameron's bedside because he wanted to talk to us. He spent the next few hours with us, observing Cameron and asking questions about my pregnancy and delivery. He questioned us regarding what tests had been performed during my pregnancy. He asked me if I had been tested for Group B Strep. I told him that I was tested and my results were negative. I also told him that I did receive all of the routine prenatal tests as well as an amnio for genetic testing purposes. Every test result was normal. There were no abnormal results at all. I remember him asking me at least two more times about being tested for Group B Strep. I again told him that I tested negative, but then I began to doubt whether or not I had received the results. I had over forty prenatal visits during my pregnancy and I was not 100% positive that I received negative results for this test; although I was 100% sure I did receive the test. He wanted the test result verified so I assured him that I would call my OB/GYN first thing the next morning to verify those results. As it turns out I was Group B Strep negative so that was not a factor in why Cameron had developed his infection. After our visit with this doctor I felt so much more hopeful about Cameron. Cam was not paralyzed. His reflexes were extremely delayed and he was very lethargic but that was understandable due to all of the medications he had been given prior to the placement of his ventilator the night before. He seemed to really care about Cameron and about us and wanted to make sure we had the opportunity to ask all of the questions that we wanted. We would later learn that this doctor was not going to be Cameron's attending pediatrician but after hearing Cameron's nurse telling another nurse about how we left that day totally shattered he decided to step in and intervene in Cameron's case. We never saw this physician again but we will be forever grateful to him for caring about our son and our family. He gave us hope when hope was lost.

By the following day Cameron was removed from the ventilator and we were able to hold our son again. Cameron was sent for a CT scan which showed a subdural hematoma (a collection of blood on the brain's surface), an injury that was attributed to birth. Even though Cameron's delivery was quite quick and unassisted, he had sustained trauma during the birth. We learned that it is not that uncommon for a newborn to suffer such trauma and that typically there are no lasting effects from the bleed. The doctor assured us that he would have no lasting effects from his hematoma. They also sent Cameron for another spinal tap. And again no fluid was obtained. Cameron's team decided that they would diagnose Cameron with suspected meningitis and he would be treated with a fourteen day course of antibiotics. Over the next several days Cameron improved. He had to re-learn how to eat (suck, swallow and breath) and how to regulate his body temperature, both of which he did quickly. And his sweet disposition again shined through. He was such a content baby; rarely did we hear him cry. The nurses all loved him because he never fussed when they changed his IV, drew blood or did anything else to him. As a result all of the nurses wanted Cameron as a patient.

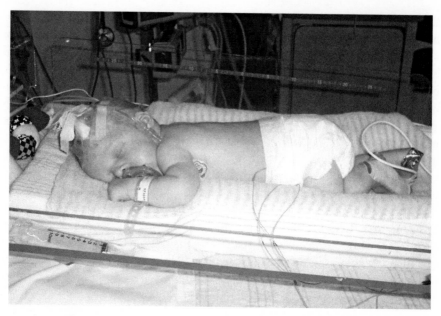

This is a picture of Cameron after the ventilator was removed.

Once Cameron was out of danger, Tim returned to work and I lived at the Ronald McDonald House during the week. Our plan was that I would come home on Friday nights and then Tim, Abby, and I would return to the hospital on Saturday for a family visit. During the week my goal was to take care of Cameron. Although I was scared, I made myself take on all of his care that the nurses would allow. And I held him day and night. I would arrive at the hospital by 6:30 am and not leave until 8 pm. Although I would leave Cam's room to send a daily e-mail to our family and friends with his updates or to grab a very quick bite to eat, the remainder of my time I spent with Cameron—just holding him and watching him. And each day he grew stronger.

After eleven of the fourteen days of antibiotics, Cameron began to fuss. His appetite substantially decreased and he became lethargic. I grew concerned as did his doctor. The decision was made to tap Cameron again. This would be his twelfth spinal tap and it needed to produce fluid. Since both hospitals had been unsuccessful in obtaining spinal fluid, his doctor wanted Cameron to undergo a guided imagery tap. The fluid would be obtained from an area closer to his spinal cord to avoid the obvious bruising from all of the other attempts. The problem was that this would require exact precision. I would have to allow them to sedate Cameron so he would not move during the procedure. Any movement could result in his spinal cord being permanently damaged. I signed the consent forms after speaking to Tim. I was scared. If we did not give consent then they were going to treat Cameron with a different twenty-one day antibiotic treatment. His doctors were recommending this tap because they would be able to rule out other types of infection. I remember walking with Cameron to the prep area and watching them sedate him. He fell into a peaceful sleep and then I walked with him and the nurse to the procedure room. I was so scared. The procedure took under fifteen minutes, but I could have sworn it was more like fifteen hours. He tolerated the procedure well and fluid was obtained and sent for testing. It would take a minimum of forty-eight hours for results. As a precaution, Cameron was started on the twenty-one day cycle of antibiotics but we were told they could be discontinued once test results were back.

The test results showed no further infection and Cameron did perk back up. Although we do not know why Cameron had begun to act sick again, he was fine and he only had one day left of his meningitis antibiotic treatment. The attending physician shared the great news with me and told me that Cameron would be going home when his treatment was complete. The day prior to his discharge, a developmental therapist came by to assess Cameron and she found that he was developmentally appropriate for his age. His NICU team also gave us great news. Cameron's subdural hematoma was resolving itself based on a repeat CT scan and Cameron would have no lasting effects from his suspected meningitis. He was discharged on seizure medicines as a precaution, but we were told that the seizure that Cameron experienced most likely was a onetime occurrence. Cameron would need to follow up with a neurologist to have a repeat EEG to check for seizure activity in one month.

Fifteen days after arriving at the hospital we took our son home. To say that Abby was thrilled to see her baby brother and mommy is an understatement. She missed us both so much. She was only nineteen months old at the time and really did not understand all that had happened. It would be a long time until Abby felt comfortable without me being within her sight. My once independent toddler clung to me. I could not leave the room without Abby asking where I was going and when I would be back. She wanted mommy to do everything for her—not DaDa. She needed me and it would take time before she felt confident that I was not going to leave her again. I felt so guilty. I had chosen to live at the hospital with Cameron because he needed me, but at the same time my nineteen month old daughter had needed me too. I took solace in knowing that any mother would have made the decision I made and knowing that Abby was well taken care of. My mom was there for her and she was showered with attention and affection while I was gone.

Needless to say, Tim and I felt like the luckiest parents in the world. Our son was home and was fine. We now could get on with ordinary life. Our daughter was thrilled to be a big sister and wore her big sister shirt with such pride. Everything was settling into place. We felt so fortunate to have two healthy children, especially considering all that both of our children had experienced in their short lives. Abby had been born prematurely but was thriving and reaching every developmental milestone ahead of time and Cameron had survived suspected meningitis. We truly felt so blessed to have two healthy children and promised ourselves to never take their health for granted.

We slowly began to adjust to life with two children under the age of two. Abby adored her baby brother and Cameron was content to watch his sister running all about the house. He loved to be held and talked to, which we did plenty of. Each evening after Abby would go to bed Tim and I would play with Cameron. We would lay him on his blanket and sit and talk to him. We would talk about what an amazing little boy we had. Cam had endured so much pain as a newborn and yet he had the sweetest disposition. You could not help but be mesmerized by him.

All is Not Well

One evening, October 30th to be exact, I noticed that Cameron was turning bluish grey beneath his nose and around his mouth. I was so scared. I showed Tim and together we decided to call his pediatrician. We were still using the same pediatrician that saw Cameron after he was born and he had assured us that he was fine; he was just a lazy baby. When we called the after-hours line, his pediatrician was on call and called us back immediately. We described what we were witnessing and his doctor told us not to be concerned. He asked if he was acting normal, which he was. I reminded him of all that Cameron had been through; the seizure, the suspected meningitis, and the subdural hematoma. Again he told me that he was fine but to call back if he turned completely blue or his breathing turned labored. Cameron did not worsen and we continued to watch him closely throughout the night. I had a feeling something was amiss but as when he was born I could not decide exactly what was wrong. That evening Tim and I did make the decision that effective November 1st we would change pediatric practices. We were not 100% satisfied with the current pediatrician and we also wanted to have a pediatrician closer to our home. Since we were in an HMO we knew that we had to notify our insurance and see what providers in our area were accepting new patients. We would ask our friends for recommendations. And if Cameron experienced another episode we decided we were heading to the ER, referral or no referral.

On Halloween Cameron was fine and we went trick or treating for a little while. When we returned home the phone rang—it was the head of the pediatric practice and he wanted to know what the doctor at the ER said the night before about Cameron's turning blue under his nose. I was shocked and told this doctor that his partner did not authorize us to go to the ER and told us that everything was fine, not to worry. I also told him that we had decided to change pediatric practices due to a sense of not feeling confident any longer in the practice. When Tim got home from work and I told him what had happened we both felt like this doctor was trying to cover their practice because he did not agree with the other pediatrician's opinion. I also called the HMO to initiate the change in our children's pediatrician. I told them how dissatisfied we were with the care we had received to date.

Cameron had another turning slightly blue episode a few days later, in early November and I immediately called the new pediatrician's office. I was told to bring Cameron right over. Abby, Cam and I were to meet with one of the pediatricians who had just joined the practice two weeks prior. I will never forget how comfortable I felt when Dr. Tjaden walked into the exam room and introduced himself. He then asked what was happening and I explained everything, including Cameron's history. He proceeded to examine Cameron. He looked concerned but remained very calm and reassuring to me. He asked if he could bring another physician in for a consult and I readily agreed. This was when we would also meet Dr. Kaufman. Dr. Kaufman and Dr. Tjaden returned to our room after a few moments and Dr. Kaufman asked some questions about Cameron's history and examined him as well. He then told me that he agreed with Dr. Tjaden's assessment of Cameron. Both pediatricians felt it was necessary for Cameron to be admitted to Advocate Lutheran General Hospital in Park Ridge, Illinois for observation and testing. They sent a nurse in to help me with Abby while they arranged for Cameron's admission. They told me they were going to try to get Cameron admitted as a patient of Dr. Nishant Shah, the director of Pediatric Neurology at Advocate Lutheran General Hospital.

Oddly, I remained completely calm. I am not sure why—maybe because the entire office staff were so friendly and helpful or maybe because I truly had no idea that that evening our lives were going to change forever. Regardless, I was calm. The office staff let me use the phone to call my mom. My mom would meet me at home to watch Abby and I would pack a quick bag for Cameron and myself. I also called Tim at work and I explained what was happening and asked him to meet me at the admitting office of the hospital. Once all of the admission arrangements were made we left the pediatrician's office and headed home. My mom looked concerned when I arrived home, but I quickly reassured her that everything was fine. Cameron was going to the hospital for additional testing and he would be home probably by the next day.

By the time Cam and I arrived at Advocate Lutheran General Hospital Tim was there and together we all walked into admitting. Cameron was admitted as a patient of Dr. Nishant Shah and we were taken to the pediatric unit. We settled into Cameron's room and a nurse came in to do the admitting paperwork and vitals. We were told that we would see Dr. Shah shortly. Since Advocate Lutheran General Hospital is a teaching hospital, we saw several residents over the course of the next hour. Each resident asked us about Cameron's birth history and prior hospital admission. They wanted to know all of the details of what led us to this admission. We did not mind repeating his story because we knew that it was part of being a patient in a teaching hospital.

Then the kindest gentleman walked in and introduced himself—it was Dr. Nishant Shah. He had a calming presence and he spoke with such sincerity. He asked about Cameron's birth, my pregnancy, and his suspected meningitis. He told us that the first two tests that he wanted to perform were a blood test to check Cameron's seizure medicine levels and an MRI to check the status of Cameron's subdural hematoma. He asked if we had any questions and assured us that if we thought of any after he left to just ask the nurse to page him. He said he would return as soon as the test results were obtained. Cameron's testing was completed within two hours. He was sedated for his MRI and after the MRI his blood was drawn while he was still under the effects of the sedation. He was cooperative as usual.

About 8 pm Tim and I were sitting in Cameron's room and figured that we would not receive any tests results until the morning. Tim was getting ready to head home to spend some time with Abby and I was going to stay with Cam. Tim was holding Cam and saying good-bye when Dr. Shah walked in and said he had the MRI results to discuss with us. We just assumed he was going to tell us that Cameron's subdural hematoma was completely dissolved. He asked us to sit down so Tim put Cameron in the hospital crib and we sat down to talk. We never expected to hear what we were about to hear. Dr. Shah started out explaining that Cameron's MRI results were available and there were some findings that he wanted to discuss with us. He was so calm and so easy to talk to. He explained that there were several areas of white matter abnormalities on Cameron's MRI. At first we did not understand that this meant that Cameron had permanent brain damage and we just listened without asking any questions. Dr. Shah must have realized we did not understand the seriousness of these findings and so he explained to us exactly what this meant. When we realized Cameron had suffered extensive brain damage we began asking question after question. We were confused how Cameron would have sustained brain damage when he had no damage upon discharge from the other hospital just a few short weeks earlier. He then explained that when a child has a serious infection, such as meningitis, sometimes the damage does not appear immediately. He also said he wanted to show us another area of concern on Cameron's MRI and he took us to a computer at the nurse's station. He showed us Cameron's brain and then explained to us that Cameron had encephalomalacia, a shrinking of the brain, again due to the infection he had shortly after birth.

Upon returning to Cameron's room I can remember that I began to cry, well actually sob. Dr. Shah sat patiently while Tim and I tried to compose ourselves. He did not make us feel uncomfortable. I then remember asking him, "What does this mean?" He said that he would not make any formal diagnosis until one year of age but the type of white matter abnormalities that he was seeing are sometimes consistent with cerebral palsy. Again we cried. When we stopped crying I began to ask, "Will Cameron walk? Will he ever talk? Will he have any quality of life?" and rather than guessing or worst yet telling us no he gave us an answer that has driven all of our efforts these past four years. Dr. Shah told us "The day you say Cameron will never do something, he never will!" Dr. Shah did not give us false hope but he gave us hope to know that no one, including himself, could predict Cameron's outcome and future abilities. Dr. Shah strongly recommended that we begin therapy immediately because with therapy we could maximize Cameron's healthy areas of his brain to help compensate for his damaged areas. He told us that when Cameron reaches one year of age if we find that he is developing right on track then nothing will have been lost by getting intervention early. However, if we take a wait and see approach we might miss an important window of opportunity to really help Cameron learn how to compensate for his deficits.

Dr. Shah spent over two hours with us that evening—letting us ask him the same questions over and over, allowing us to cry without making us feel like we were imposing on his time. From that first meeting we knew that he would be an important part of our family's life. He gave us hope when many other physicians would not have. When Dr. Shah left, Tim and I were absolutely exhausted. Tim did head home to spend the evening with Abby and I remained at the hospital with Cam. We did not talk about the MRI results. We just hugged and said goodnight. After Tim left I held my son and cried. I cried harder than I had ever cried in my life. The uncertainty of his future was unbearable. I have always been a control freak and there was nothing about Cameron that I was able to control. That was the hardest thing for me to accept. No matter what I did I had no control over what had already happened to Cameron.

Tim returned to the hospital the next morning and we sat and talked. Both of us were in shock and disbelief about the MRI results we heard the day before. Cameron looked too good to be so sick. Neither of us knew anyone with cerebral palsy but we had both seen stories of children with severe cerebral palsy. We had no idea that there were varying degrees of severity. Together, we decided that we would not tell our family or friends what we had just found out. We did not want anyone to give up hope on Cameron. We decided to tell them that Dr. Shah wanted to be proactive and start Cameron in therapy due to how sick he was as a newborn. Luckily, Cameron's blood work showed that he had outgrown his dose of seizure meds so we were able to emphasize that news when we spoke to inquiring family members and friends. We took Cameron home knowing we were being so dishonest with everyone around us. But, we were not yet ready to face the opinions and advice of others. We did feel very confident in Dr. Shah and felt completely comfortable with his diagnostic skills. Looking back I think one reason we chose to keep the news a secret at first was because if we started to tell people then it would have meant it was really true. We were not quite ready to accept the fact that our son had extensive brain damage.

The month of November and most of December were terrible. Each night I cried myself to sleep wondering what the future would hold for Cameron and our family. Tim and I began to talk about selling our home since it was not handicapped accessible and moving into a ranch house that Cameron would be able to live more comfortably in as he got older and too big for us to carry. For a few weeks we felt truly hopeless. We did not talk about the possibility that Cameron would be able to walk, talk, etc. Rather we let our minds take us into darkness and we started to assume that he would never do these things.

One December evening I was taking my mom and the kids to my niece's birthday party and I got lost. As I drove around and could not find my way I started to get so angry I was screaming and yelling. My mom started to yell back at me and said what is wrong with you? You are not yourself lately. What is going on? It is then that I stopped the car and angrily told her all that we knew about Cameron. I was swearing, crying and yelling. I felt completely out of control and completely alone. I remember her telling me that Cameron would be okay because we would do everything the doctor said. And I remember telling her that she was wrong, that he would never be okay. I ended up dropping her off at the birthday party and driving home crying. I still do not know exactly how I made it home. When I got home the phone rang and it was my brother. He was all upset at me for not coming to the party. I just told him that he had no idea what was going on and to leave me alone. I hung up the phone and cried the night away. When Tim got home that evening I told him what had happened and apologized for telling my mom. He was actually relieved. He said we needed to reach out for support from our families and that keeping this secret was tearing us apart.

Around that time we went back for a follow-up visit with Dr. Shah. Again, Dr. Shah was so positive and so encouraging. We told him about our fears and again he told us "The day you say Cameron will never do something, he never will." He went on to tell us that he has patients with extensive brain damage that have excellent physical and cognitive abilities, and he has patients with minimal damage that have very little physical and cognitive abilities. He explained to us that if we began therapy immediately we could help Cameron's brain learn to do things in a different way due to the damaged areas. Cameron could potentially learn to walk, talk, etc. He emphasized the importance of starting therapy immediately. He explained that a baby has the ability to maximize those areas of the brain that are healthy more so than an adult who suffers brain damage would be able to. When we left this visit Tim and I felt hopeful.

At the suggestion of Dr. Shah, we contacted Options and Advocacy (O & A) of McHenry County. O&A provides Early Intervention services to children from birth to three years of age who are at risk for developmental delays. Children are eligible to receive Early Intervention services if they have an eligible medical diagnosis (such as cerebral palsy or Down syndrome) or if they are 30% or more delayed in any area of development as determined by evaluations. I spoke with the intake coordinator who arranged for Cameron to receive the evaluations that would be necessary for him to begin therapy.

The Start of Therapy and Hopefulness Returns

The holidays passed and Cameron's evaluations were completed. Due to a significant delay, Cameron qualified to receive physical therapy. We were fortunate to live only ten minutes from a therapy center. I will never forget the day that I took Cameron to his first physical therapy appointment. I was so scared and yet so hopeful. His physical therapist would be Dolores. From the moment I met Dolores I felt confident that she was going to push Cameron to maximize his physical abilities. Since Cameron was just four months old I would attend his physical therapy (PT) sessions with him.

The first few months were hard. He would cry throughout the session and constantly want me to hold him. It was hard to listen to him cry and yet I knew it was what I needed to do. Many times I left Cameron's sessions in tears myself and I would call Tim from the cell phone for support. We were given exercises to work on at home between sessions and together we worked on them as much as we could. We tried to make the exercises fun and encouraged Abby to help us as much as possible. Over time, Cameron did start to show improvement. He had very little trunk control when we began therapy and Dolores explained that we needed to improve his trunk control before he would be able to successfully sit up, pull to stand and someday walk.

There were times that Cameron made progress quickly and I would feel happier and somewhat myself again. But then he would plateau in his progress and I would feel my mood slip. I would notice myself crying more often and for longer periods of time. It was truly an emotional rollercoaster. There were days that I do not remember how I dragged myself out of bed and cared for my two small children, but somehow I did it. I tried to maintain as normal of a routine as possible for Abby's sake. She had been through so many changes already and she needed to have a sense of normalcy.

Here are some pictures of Cam working hard on his physical therapy exercises. Dolores, his physical therapist, emphasized during many sessions how important it was for Cam to strengthen his abdominal muscles (his core area) because a strong core would enable him to sit and would also allow him to have the ability to use his arms and legs. The first picture shows Cam hanging out while Tim does some exercises with him on the therapy ball at home. Abby loved to bounce on the therapy ball—she would giggle and giggle! A lot of times Cam would just suck his thumb and wait for the exercises to be done. The therapy ball was also a lot of work, so Cam was always happy when it was Abby's turn! The second picture is a recent picture (May 2008) of Cam with Dolores during a therapy session. Cam loves the swing and he loves that he now gets to stand on it too!

Unconditional Love—Abby's Gift

Each day I watched in amazement at the unconditional love that Abby had for her brother. Every day she would tell him how much she loved him and that he was her best friend. Never once did she see him as anything but Cameron. He was her brother and she loved him. I also watched as she befriended the different children we met at therapy. She was never afraid to go up to a child in a wheelchair or speak to a child with cerebral palsy, Down syndrome or autism. Actually, it was quite the opposite. She took delight in meeting all of these children and always asked about them when they were missing from the center. Never once did she see their disability. She saw each child for who they really were. She also made friends with Donna, the receptionist at the therapy center. Donna was such a source of support for both Abby and I. On tough days she would give me a hug and listen as I talked. When Cameron reached a milestone she would celebrate with us. And she made Abby feel so special. She would stock the candy jar with Abby's favorite suckers or chocolates. She would ask Abby about her friends and her favorite things to do. When Abby drew her a picture she would hang it for everyone to see. One day Abby made me so proud. I asked her what she wanted to be when she grew up and she told me that she wanted to be Donna. I asked her why and she said because she is a friend to everyone at therapy and makes everyone feel so happy. I told her that if she grows up to be just like Donna I would be so very proud of her. Donna is one amazing woman who truly helped me through some of my darkest moments in this journey of ours.

Abby grew very attached to each of Cameron's therapists and was very interested in what they would do during a session with him. She was very imaginative and often times when she would play with her dolls I would overhear her talking. At times her dolls had cerebral palsy or asthma and she would be reassuring them that they were doing very well and that she was going to help them to learn to walk, talk or to breathe better. I found it very fascinating to sit and listen to her conversations because I was able to see that the openness that we had about Cameron and his special needs eliminated the fear that Abby might have felt if we hid some of the information from her. She was able to understand what he was experiencing and how with patience and time you can sometimes help someone to overcome challenges. I do believe that her ability to engage in this type of pretend play was an important factor in the development of her unconditional love for Cam.

Abby loved to hold Cameron, but as you can
see she was really not much bigger than he was!

Finding My Voice—Becoming Cameron's Advocate

Well it finally happened. I finally gathered up my courage to speak up and be Cameron's advocate. Until now when I did not like the manner in which a physician or other medical professional treated Cameron or our family I chose to walk away from the situation and remedy it by finding alternate care for Cameron.

The first instance of not finding my voice occurred after Cameron's birth. As I mentioned earlier, Cameron did not cry after he was born. He did not cry during his circumcision and it was noted in his hospital chart that he was lethargic and lacked any type of reaction to painful stimuli. I voiced my concerns about what a lethargic baby Cameron was after he was born and while we were still in the hospital. Both times his former pediatrician told me "Mom, he is a full-term baby, full-term babies are not colicky like your daughter was (Abby was a preemie)." I did not feel comfortable with his response and yet he was firm and direct. I took Cam home and still felt something was amiss but I did not have any proof that anything was wrong. My husband and I even took Cameron in to see the pediatrician after Cam's first weekend home. We were concerned because Cameron was yellowish in color and he was not waking for feedings and was still very lethargic. Again the pediatrician dismissed our concerns and told us that Cameron was just fine. We should be happy to have a baby who was already sleeping through the night considering that many new parents wait months for that to happen. I wish I would have insisted that I see another one of the pediatricians in the practice or have blood work drawn. Instead, Tim and I took Cameron home. We complied with the pediatrician's answers about Cam's lethargic disposition. Of course, we would soon learn that the reason why Cameron was so lethargic was due to a raging infection within his body. If only we would have insisted on a second opinion or been more assertive and not accepted an easy answer from that pediatrician, how different all of our lives might be. Unfortunately, if only's do not change things and can lead to much anger and an inability to accept what is currently happening.

Another instance of not finding my voice occurred after Cam was placed on a ventilator and emergency transported to a Chicago area hospital. The following morning, the neurologist assigned to Cameron spent five minutes with Tim and I and told us that we had made a mistake by allowing Cameron to be placed on a ventilator because now if he survived he would have no brain functionality and no worthwhile life. I never found the courage to later tell this physician that the manner in which he was delivering devastating news to us was inappropriate. Standing in the middle of the NICU talking to us about our son without bothering to learn our names or Cameron's name was impersonal. Without any diagnostic tests to back up what he was saying he was unjustified in making such blanket statements. And regardless of what he felt was a worthwhile life, this was our son, we wanted him and we were going to do everything we could to keep him alive. I never found my voice. After Cameron made a turn around and was discharged from this hospital my solution was that he would no longer receive neurological care there. I spoke to Tim and together we agreed that the next follow-up that Cameron would require by a neurologist would be done at another institution. We also made the same decision with regard to the pediatric practice we were using. Unfortunately, I did not write a letter or place a call to the pediatric practice manager or the hospital administrator to notify either of the poor medical care Cameron had received. I did not have the courage within myself to do that. After all, I was only Cameron's mom. I had no formal medical training and certainly not a M.D. behind my name to warrant any type of respect from either of these physicians. Today, I do not feel that way at all. I am Cameron's mom and I am committed to helping him become everything that he can be. I will voice my concerns to any medical professional who I feel is not listening to me. After all, Cameron's life depends on me being his advocate as I have learned the hard way. And my voice has value. As Cameron's mom, I know him better than anyone else. I pick up on things that a physician might miss. This is the main reason why Cameron's entire medical team has been chosen, because they approach his care as a team approach. Cameron, Tim and I are equally as important and respected members of this team as each of the medical professionals are. After all, a team is only as strong as its' weakest link, fortunately this team has no weak links. Additionally, as members need to be added to Cam's team they will have to be willing to work within this team model. Everything we have done for Cameron since meeting Dr. Nishant Shah has worked for Cameron so we will continue to work within this model of care that we have all worked so hard to fine tune and customize to meet Cameron's needs.

I found my voice in June of 2004, when Cameron was nine months old. Cameron's physical therapist, Dolores, had noted that Cameron would not bear any weight on his left foot. He would curl his foot inward due to his increased muscle tone. Dolores shared with me that the main concern she had was that if Cameron learned to stand or walk with his left foot in this position that the muscles on the outer part of his foot would not be strengthened and in the future he might have problems with joints wearing improperly due to misuse. Her recommendation was to see an orthopedic surgeon to receive a prescription for a type of foot brace called an AFO. It would be a plastic molded brace that would be completely enclosed within Cameron's shoe to force him to stand properly on his left foot. Cameron's pediatrician agreed with Dolores' assessment and gave us a referral to see an area orthopedic surgeon that was in our HMO plan.

On June 24th, I took Cameron to see Dr. O. My twelve-year-old niece, Rachel, was visiting and she came with me to the appointment to help watch Abby as I spoke to the doctor. To say the appointment went poorly is an understatement. From the moment Dr. O walked into the examination room until the moment he left I was given no opportunity to express my concerns about Cameron's foot. Each time I attempted to talk, Dr. O interrupted me. It was frustrating and when we left Rachel said "Auntie, the doctor never even let you finish a sentence." I said I know and that I was very unhappy with the statements he made. After I arrived home I was angry. Angry by the entire visit as well as the attitude of Dr. O I decided that we would take Cameron to another orthopedic surgeon to assess his foot. I also decided to take a proactive step and address the manner in which Dr. O conducted the visit as well as what he said to me. I decided to write a letter to Dr. O and I felt very empowered as I signed and mailed the letter. I voiced my concerns and felt like maybe Dr. O would read this letter and understand that he had not listened to my concerns and further had criticized our treatment approach (providing a young child with a brain injury with therapy in order to maximize a child's abilities) without regard for the fact that we were following a standard of care for a child with a brain injury. I gave a copy of the letter to Dolores and Cam's pediatrician. Both applauded me for speaking up and voicing my concerns in a professional manner.

Imagine my surprise, when a few days later, a letter from Dr. O arrived at our home. My reaction to his letter was that I was in complete and utter shock. I could not believe that Dr. O wrote to tell me that I needed to challenge Cameron's doctors and therapists regarding their treatment decisions. The treatment decisions made by Cameron's medical team were sound and were working. They were made based on scientific research that proves the benefits of providing a child with a brain injury with Early Intervention services in order to maximize the child's abilities. If the letter was not enough to shock me what was enclosed was. Dr. O enclosed a three page article in which he highlighted a few key statements that he felt supported his beliefs. The problem that I had with this article was that it was three pages from a textbook; there was no date for the materials and no reference as to the actual source of the information for me to further research what he sent to me. I decided to not write Dr. O back or to respond further. He obviously was determined to have the final say and I let him. I felt so empowered in terms of my ability though to address my concerns with Dr. O and to make the decision to seek another orthopedic surgeon's opinion.

More Therapy, More Progress

When Cameron was nine months old we were advised to add developmental therapy (DT) to his schedule. The recommendation was to have Cameron receive DT once a month. We were assigned a developmental therapist by the name of Jamie who made monthly visits to our house. She talked about teaching Cameron appropriate play techniques and began working on having Cameron build blocks rather than bang them, shake rattles rather than only mouth them, etc. She would also provide me with ideas for activities to do with both Abby and Cameron.

Cameron also began weekly occupational therapy (OT) with Robin. Robin explained that in addition to Cameron working on his gross motor skills we now also needed to focus on his fine motor skills. Fine motor skills would later be important for Cameron to learn to self feed, play with toys with small pieces and to write. Robin also would help work on some of the slight sensory issues we were beginning to notice with Cameron, such as his oversensitivity to certain food textures and tastes, avoidance of touching certain textures and his undersensitivity to noise.

As we added more therapy to Cameron's schedule, I found myself busier and busier with Cameron. It gave me a little less time to sit and worry about the delays I was noticing and rather focus on all of the help we were able to give to him. Plus, I found that the two additional therapists that became part of our lives, Jamie and Robin, were really great support people to me. I felt comfortable opening up, sharing my fears with them and asking them for advice. I found that just by talking about my worries I felt better. Sometimes getting something out in the open rather than keeping it bottled up inside was helpful. Plus, both Jamie and Robin had experience working with many children and their families. They were able to provide me with the support I needed. Often times they assured me that my worries were normal, that other parents of children with special needs also worried about the same things. And they were able to give me practical suggestions for working with Cameron but also for how to help Abby through the medical situations we were experiencing and the sibling jealousy that sometimes arose due to all of the time that we had to spend getting Cameron the help he needed. I can honestly say that although adding additional visits to our weekly schedule presented some scheduling challenges at times, the benefits of seeing Cameron make progress and receiving more support myself far outweighed the scheduling logistics.

Wishing Away Cameron's First Year

Throughout Cameron's first year we were very busy with therapy sessions, visits to the pediatrician and Dr. Shah. In the back of my mind I think that I wished away Cameron's first year of life. I needed to know his diagnosis—did he have cerebral palsy or not. Once I knew I told myself I could heal and move on. Sadly, I look back and regret not enjoying each of Cameron's firsts more. I was so overwhelmed by his potential diagnosis that I forgot to stop and let myself truly savor the moment we were in. Instead, a milestone reached represented a new goal—to work as hard as we could to reach the next milestone. I do remember each of Cameron's firsts but with a degree of extremeness. My life revolved around therapy, exercises and working towards the next milestone. It was all about working harder, not enjoying the moments more.

It was also a difficult year because our lives changed so much. I was no longer able to do as much with Abby. Abby missed numerous music classes, play dates and chances to be a toddler because of therapy visits and doctor appointments. She never complained, she just went with the flow. But I felt so guilty. Every ounce of my energy was spent on Cameron and there was little extra for Abby. Occasionally, I was able to capture some alone time with Abby and we savored the time we had. One of our favorite things to do was to go to Einstein Bagels. Abby loved sitting there eating her bagel, talking with her mommy and people watching. And I thoroughly enjoyed her company. It was a break from the increasing pressure I felt caring for Cameron. I now realize that I often refused when others offered to help with Cameron because I thought it was my sole responsibility to take care of him. I did not think that anyone else would care for him like I did and as a result I tried to do it all myself. I would later learn that I did not have the ability to care for Cam alone and that it was not only beneficial to me but to Cam and our family to allow others to help.

As Cameron's birthday approached I found myself very busy planning his 1st birthday party. It was hard to believe that he was turning one and I wanted to plan a big celebration similar to what we planned for Abby. We invited over ninety people to a pirate themed birthday party for Cam and over eighty people attended. We hosted the party at a local children's pirate theme park. I made all of his invitations and even found a pirate costume for Cam to wear to greet his guests as they arrived. There was a time when we thought we would not be celebrating this huge milestone and I wanted to make sure we celebrated in style. The party was awesome and everyone was amazed by how healthy and strong Cameron looked. Cameron had mastered sitting up and had recently started to crawl a bit, so we were proud to show off all of his new abilities to everyone.

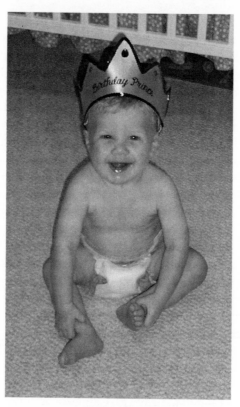

Cam on the morning of his 1st Birthday ...
Our Birthday Prince!

A family picture at Cameron's 1ˢᵗ Birthday Party. Here he is in his pirate outfit and Abby proudly wore her "I'm the Big Sister!" shirt.

After Cameron's party was over the reality of Cameron's potential diagnosis hit us hard. We would be seeing Dr. Shah after having a repeat MRI and we were nervous. Although we spent the year preparing for a diagnosis of cerebral palsy, we were scared to finally have an answer. Needless to say when we saw Dr. Shah he was impressed by Cameron and he remarked at how strong Cameron appeared. Dr. Shah was so happy to see the progress that he had made. He told us the criteria that he would use to diagnose Cameron and after reviewing his MRI and performing an exam, he did diagnose Cameron with cerebral palsy.

Again Dr. Shah assured us that having this diagnosis did not change the fact that Cameron was making such great progress and that with continued therapy he expected to see more progress. He reminded us that although Cameron was diagnosed with cerebral palsy that Cameron was still Cameron. He was not cerebral palsy; he was an amazing little boy who just happened to have cerebral palsy. That was such a powerful statement and really was something I needed to hear. I remember when Cameron was about 5 months old and a health care provider addressed Cameron as the CP (cerebral palsy) patient. I was so angry. I told this provider that Cam was not the CP patient, rather he was a boy named Cameron who might happen to have cerebral palsy. I do not remember anything else about that visit and we never saw that provider again. I think that when I heard the diagnosis that was my biggest fear, that all of a sudden our son would be seen only for his disability and not for all that he is. I was deter-mined to make sure that he was never referred to as a diagnosis again. Rather, he is Cameron. He is an extraordinary, amazing little boy who has overcome so much in his short life, and yes, he just so happens to have cerebral palsy.

Again Tim and I were silent in our thoughts as we drove home from Cameron's appointment. We had spent the past nine months preparing to hear this diagnosis and yet we were completely unprepared to hear it, if that makes any sense. When we sat down to talk about how we felt we both admitted we felt a sense of sadness for Cameron. We felt so guilty and we both wondered if we had missed some sign after his birth to indicate how sick he was. If only we would have done this or that … would Cameron not have had to endure all that he had during his first year of life? We felt so sorry for him. Sorry that he had to work so hard to accomplish milestones that his sister and his peers reached effortlessly. We wondered about his future. After a few sad days we decided that we were not helping Cameron at all. He did not want us to feel sorry for him. He was the happiest little boy and he was alive. He deserved for us to celebrate, not grieve, his life. And Abby deserved for us to celebrate her brother's life. Cameron joining our family had changed our lives forever and for the better. I sat down and wrote Cameron the following letter for his first birthday.

Cameron,

I cannot even believe that you are turning One! To say that this past year has just flown by is such an understatement. It seems like just yesterday I was holding my newborn son in my arms and just looking at each and every detail about you with amazement. From the moment the doctor handed you to me I was smitten by your beautiful smile and glistening eyes. You were so calm and relaxed. You just looked up at me with complete trust and from that moment on I knew we were going to be an awesome team. Loving you came so easy and naturally not only to me, but to your big sister Abby and your DaDa as well. Every time you looked at any of us our hearts just melted. You had such a calming presence about you. Your arrival made our family complete.

Throughout this first year I have watched you fight so hard to survive. When you became sick at one week of age and we were told that you might not survive, my heart just stopped. Although we had only had you in our lives for 1 week, the thought of not having you anymore was too much to bear. You proved everyone wrong though—to say that you are strong is an understatement. The will to live that you showed was amazing. Every day in the hospital you grew stronger and stronger—as if you knew that if you got better you would be coming back home to our family again.

Having you in my life this past year has been such an amazing journey. I have watched you defy the odds more than once and work so incredibly hard to accomplish each of your milestones. I have had to watch you cry through therapy sessions and cheer you on when all the while I cried in my heart to want to let you stop. But I knew that what we were doing was in your best interest. And I have watched you emerge as an independent toddler after months of hard work. I will never forget the moment I saw you first roll over, sit up and crawl. I cried as you reached each of these milestones, but the tears were tears of joy.

In just one year you have taught me what many people never learn—that if you want something bad enough you can achieve it through determination and lots of hard work. You have made me realize that any obstacle in life can be overcome. You have also taught me that what truly does matter is the kind of person you are—it does not matter what you can or cannot do—but it matters how you treat others and how they treat you. This year we have needed to ask for help from so many people—and this is the first time in my life that I have had to do that.

I have had to admit that I cannot always do everything by myself. The amazing part of this is that we had so many people in our lives that cared enough about us that they were more than willing to help. And the support that we received was not only from family members, but from very good friends. I have learned this past year that it does not matter the quantity of friends that you have, but rather the quality of friends. I have been blessed to have some very true friends, friends who have cried with me, laughed with me and just offered to listen when I needed to talk.

I am so happy to be your mommy Cameron. I look forward to watching you grow and become a strong, independent young man. I have no doubt in my mind that each and every person that you encounter will have their lives touched in a special way by you. I hope that all that you do you find success in but even more I hope that you have true happiness in your life.

Thank you so much for making this past year an incredible year for me—this year has been filled with more love and happiness than I would have ever imagined possible. I love you with all of my heart Cameron!
Love,
Mommy

A Cruise for Mommy and DaDa—or Not?

The second year of Cameron's life brought different challenges for our family. We had adjusted to Cameron's therapy schedule and we had also adjusted to having two children. We were excited to see Cameron making daily improvements and watching his love for Abby grow each day. We watched him watch her and want to be just like her. He seemed to be intent on keeping up with his sister. When Abby would sit down to play with him he smiled so big. He watched her as if he was trying to learn from her how to move. He would look for her when she was not around. And he started to seem almost bored with us when she was gone. He loved her constant attention.

Cameron was looking so healthy to us and I was really feeling more confident in his health. Tim and I decided that it was time for us to take a small vacation alone. We had been through so much and we needed a chance to spend time alone, just the two of us. My mom agreed to stay with Abby and Cameron and Tim's parents agreed to help each day. We planned a five day cruise for October. We did buy the trip insurance as a just in case measure, but never intended to use it. I began writing down all of Cameron's information for my mom: a medical history, his doctor's information, directions to the pediatrician and a medical consent form for both Abby and Cameron.

About three weeks before our trip Cameron had his one year check-up. Due to how sick he was during his first year of life Dr. Tjaden recommended that Cameron receive the flu shot. We agreed that it would be a good idea. Abby was placed on a waiting list since there was a vaccine shortage. She was not able to get her shot until all of the patients who were at high risk received their dose. A few days after Cameron received his flu shot he had a dry cough throughout the night. I checked on him several times but he was sleeping just fine. The next day he continued to have a dry cough but no fever. Abby wanted to go to the mall so we headed to the mall to walk around for a little while. Cameron cried constantly in the car and for the hour we were at the mall, so we headed home.

When we got home I decided to call the pediatrician. The nurse scheduled an appointment for Cameron for that afternoon to have his cough checked but told me to call if his cough worsened. I put him down on the floor to play with Abby while I made lunch. Instead of playing, Cameron laid on the floor next to Abby. I figured he was tired from all of his crying but that was not the case. Within minutes I noticed that Cam's breathing was growing labored. His entire body was moving as he struggled to breathe. I quickly called 911 and then called my mom to come and watch Abby. My mom was not home so I called a neighbor of ours and she came right over to stay with Abby. By the time the ambulance arrived I was crying. I was so afraid. Cameron was struggling to breathe and I was getting very worried. His oxygen level was in the 80's. The paramedics started a nebulizer treatment and we prepared to leave for the hospital. As we were getting into the ambulance my mom pulled up. She was driving by and saw the ambulance. My mom and our neighbor stayed with Abby. I also asked my mom to call Tim at work and tell him to meet us at the hospital. The nebulizer treatment that the paramedics gave Cameron did not improve his breathing at all. They then started to administer oxygen.

When we arrived at the hospital the ER physician ordered an immediate chest x-ray and began a continuous nebulizer treatment for Cameron. Cam's oxygen level was still in the 80's (should be high 90's if not 100) and he was not improving at all. The chest x-ray showed that Cameron had pneumonia. Due to Cameron's medical history the ER physician decided that Cameron needed to be transported to a children's hospital and after consulting with Dr. Tjaden the decision to have the Advocate Lutheran General Children's Hospital medical transport team pick Cameron up was made. While we waited for the transport team to arrive the ER physician began discussing the possibility of placing Cameron on a ventilator. Of course I started to cry. I told him we could not do that because we had come too far with Cam and if we had him ventilated again we would be starting all over. Luckily, they did not ventilate Cameron.

When the transport team arrived, they quickly assessed Cameron and then told us what to expect in terms of his transport. They also let us know that I could not ride along in the ambulance because that was hospital policy. They told Tim and I to drive carefully and that they would meet us in the pediatric intensive care unit (PICU). It was rush hour and traffic was terrible. We kissed Cameron good-bye and watched the ambulance leave. The drive was so hard. We talked about his last transport and worried about whether they would ventilate him or not during the transport. It took us over an hour and a half to get to the hospital. I felt like I was reliving every moment and every emotion of Cameron's last transport.

By the time we arrived in the PICU I was scared. I saw the transport physician as we entered the unit and I immediately asked if Cameron survived the transport. He did survive but he was in serious condition. They were getting him set up in his room and then we would be allowed to join him. They determined that he did not have pneumonia but rather he was experiencing a severe asthma attack that was causing his left lung to collapse. The plan was to give Cameron 24 hours of continuous nebulizer treatments and then to re-assess his status. Once Cameron was all settled into his room, Tim and I joined him. We were so happy to hold him.

We also called home and we had the chance to talk to Abby. She was so scared and kept asking us if Cameron was okay. She was very upset. I decided to go home for the evening while Tim would stay overnight with Cameron. It was such a hard decision to make. Up until now, I was the one who stayed overnight in the hospital with Cameron. I was the one who had to have control over the situation. But Abby needed me so much. I could hear it in her voice. And Tim assured me that he would call me immediately if anything changed with Cameron. So I went home and Abby was thrilled to see her mommy. She slept in our bed that night and in the morning we read books and then went to Einstein Bagels for breakfast. After breakfast I dropped her off at my mom's house and returned to the hospital.

Tim and Cameron had a pretty rough night. Cameron would not wear the nebulizer mask so Tim held Cameron all night with the mask near his face. He said Cameron was pretty agitated. Cameron's breathing had stabilized and by evening they decided to move him to a regular room of the pediatric unit. They also decided to space his treatments out to every four hours. Cameron's breathing continued to improve. Cameron was discharged the following day on a flovent inhaler. He would require treatments twice a day. He was also discharged on an albuterol inhaler. We were to use the albuterol inhaler whenever Cameron experienced any breathing difficulties. We were told to keep Cameron away from anyone sick because it was critical to keep him healthy for the next 6 weeks in order to give his lungs a chance to heal. Also, we were told to have Cameron tested for allergies. The only thing that had happened prior to Cameron's severe asthma attack was that he was given the flu shot, so the attending physician wondered if Cameron had any allergies.

We were told to follow up with the director of pediatric pulmonology at Advocate Lutheran General Hospital, Dr. Aljadeff. We decided to cancel our vacation because there was no way we felt comfortable leaving Cameron knowing how quickly and how severely his breathing had been affected. My mom and Tim's parents were relieved. All three agreed that they would be very nervous to have us away in case Cameron suffered another severe asthma attack. Due to Cameron's hospitalization, we were able to redeem our trip insurance and we decided we could try to go on vacation again the next year.

I scheduled Cameron's allergy testing and was surprised to learn that Cameron has a severe egg, peanut and tree nut (cashew, almond, walnut, pecan are the most common) allergy. Cameron also has a slight wheat, apple, soy and milk allergy. His egg, peanut and tree nut allergies were so severe that the allergist had to give him Benadryl and monitor him in the office for an hour after testing. We were told that due to the severity of his egg allergy Cameron could never receive a flu shot again. His allergist believed that the severe asthma attack that Cam had suffered a few weeks earlier was due to the flu shot. We were also sent home with a prescription for an EpiPen (auto-injector of epinephrine administered for emergency treatment for a life threatening allergic reaction). We did not realize how serious a food allergy could be until we talked with Cameron's allergist. We knew we would have to have a peanut and tree nut free home immediately.

Grocery shopping became very challenging because so many items are manufactured in a plant that processes peanuts and/or tree nuts. We had not had any problems with food allergy reactions previously because Cameron was not interested in eating. He primarily drank his formula and had little to no interest in baby food. He was not an enthusiastic eater as his sister had been. We attributed his disinterest to having been so sick. Little did we know that part of it might have been attributed to severe food allergies. Later we would also learn that Cameron was very tongue tied, which also contributed to feeding difficulties.

Due to the severity of Cameron's food allergies, Tim and I decided that our house would be a safe food environment for Cameron. We would have no food that contained peanuts or tree nuts (including items that were processed in a factory that processes peanuts/nuts). We also would only have items where egg was not listed as the first three ingredients on their label based on Cam's allergist recommendations. Although this would limit what we would have in our house, the limits were worth it if it meant that we would not be putting Cameron into a life-threatening situation. During his short lifetime, Cameron had already survived being placed on a ventilator as well as a PICU stay due to a severe allergic reaction. We were not willing to risk his life in any way. Our goal was to never have to use the EpiPen. Yes, we would have it with us at all times, but we did not want to have Cameron have a reaction that required it. There was no guarantee that it would work and we were not willing to risk finding out.

Since Cameron was becoming more mobile and showing some interest in food, Tim and I decided to send an e-mail to our family and close friends to explain the seriousness of Cameron's food allergies and to request that they let us know if any dishes with peanut or tree nuts were going to be served at a holiday or get together. We stated that due to the life-threatening nature of Cam's allergies we would not be able to attend a function if those items would be present. We did ask to be notified before the function so that we could make alternative plans and that if we showed up at a function with peanuts or tree nuts present we would have to leave. We wanted to avoid that from happening because we knew that it would disappoint Abby to arrive at a holiday or family gathering only to realize we would have to leave immediately. Tim and I felt our requests were reasonable. We said we completely understood if the decision was made to serve these items but to give us notice so we could make alternate plans. Due to the seriousness of the situation we were confident that everyone would respect our request. Of course time would tell and tell it did!

Cameron's lungs recovered and we spent the winter free of any colds or upper respiratory problems. Cameron had ear tubes placed in November (he was fourteen months old) as well as a procedure to eliminate his tongue tied condition. After several ear infections and his questionable hearing screening results the decision was made to have tubes placed in Cameron's ears. He did have standing fluid and so the potential for additional infections and possible hearing damage existed. Cameron was watched very closely in recovery due to his asthma but his recuperation went perfectly and Cameron was sent home the same day

New Walking Shoes—$45.36 … Watching You Walk—Absolutely Priceless!

Cameron continued to do very well in physical therapy. I was ready to buy his first pair of walking shoes. Dolores (Cameron's physical therapist) told me that we could wait to buy his shoes because he would outgrow them quickly and we did not have to have them until he was confidently walking. I, however, needed for us to buy him his shoes. Buying Cam his shoes represented a milestone that I waited so long for and it helped to energize us to keep encouraging Cameron to work hard in therapy. So Tim, Abby, Cam and I went to Stride Rite one Sunday afternoon and Cameron actually slept through his shoe fitting. He did wake up after we had his new shoes on him. He just looked at them. They were as white as could be and they had small blue dinosaurs on the back. They cost $45.36, the best money we had ever spent. . He then played with Abby at one of the standing toys. Abby wanted new shoes too so we bought her a new pair of gym shoes. Even though Abby did not need a new pair of shoes it was another example of money well spent because her shoes represented her ongoing commitment to walking hand in hand with Cameron through his journey.

In November of 2004, at fourteen months of age, Cam began to pull himself up to stand and in early December he was cruising furniture. We could not believe how motivated he was to walk. He seemed so content to sit for so long that it was so much fun to see his enthusiasm shine through. He was growing stronger every day. His legs were able to bear his weight and he was standing for longer periods of time. Each evening when Tim would come home from work we would help Cameron practice walking between us and to Abby by holding his little hands. As he walked we would all cheer very enthusiastically. Of course Cameron loved the attention. He would smile and laugh. We knew he was going to walk independently some day, but we had no idea how quickly that would happen.

Around this same time Dolores decided that Cameron should come into the therapy room alone. He was depending on me too much for comfort during his sessions. Anytime he would have to do some hard work he would cry so that I would hold him for comfort. It was hard for me to let Cameron go into the therapy room alone but I agreed that it might help him. He was almost 15 months old and he did need to have a little independence.

On December 9th Cameron went in to therapy alone. For forty-five minutes Abby kept asking me when we could go in and see Cameron. She did not like the idea of waiting outside for Cameron. About fifteen minutes before the end of his session Abby and I walked into the therapy room. Cameron did not see us. He had his back to us. We stood there and watched in amazement as Cameron proceeded to walk across the entire therapy room on his own—at least thirty steps. Of course I welled up with tears and just started to cry. This is the moment I had waited to witness since we began therapy. It was so amazing to stand back and watch my little boy walking independently. Dolores said that Cameron had done this three additional times before we entered the room. I was also crying because as I watched Cameron walking across the room, Abby was cheering him on. She could not have been a more proud big sister. She ran over and hugged him so hard he fell down onto his butt and they both started to laugh. Of course I cried even harder.

When I was able to compose myself, Dolores started to talk to me. She said that Cameron was doing so amazingly well that she was going to recommend that we decrease therapy to twice a month starting in January. I agreed, but also felt sad. Physical therapy had become such a big part of our life. I knew in my heart it was the right thing to do. Cameron was ready to be a typical toddler and he did not need to be at therapy any more than what was necessary. As I stood talking with Dolores, I started to cry. I sat down and just cried and cried. Dolores asked me what was wrong and I explained to her that up until this point I had only worried about whether Cameron would be able to do certain physical things—would he sit, would he crawl, would he walk. Now I did not need to worry about that and something more important came to my mind—was Cameron going to be okay cognitively. Would he ever learn to talk, say his name and know his alphabet? I was so worried about his physical development all along that I did not stop and let myself think about his cognitive development. For some reason it hit me all at once. Would Cameron be okay cognitively?

Dolores sat down and we talked about my concerns. She also said that it was time to enjoy Cameron's moment, his accomplishment, and that I would have plenty of time to worry about his cognitive development. I again composed myself and when Abby, Cameron and I left therapy the three of us all hugged. I was so proud of Cameron and Abby and I decided that I wanted to enjoy this miraculous moment.

In the car I called Tim at work but rather than leave him a voice mail message I decided to ask the receptionist to page Tim. When Tim answered the page, he sounded concerned. I wasn't even thinking that he might think something was wrong. I quickly assured him everything was okay, actually everything was great, and explained to him what had happened at therapy—that Cameron was walking independently. He was very excited. He was so happy that he started to cry. He explained to me that although he always believed that Cameron would walk he could not believe that Cameron was walking.

It was a time to celebrate. After we got home I called everyone, including my mom, other family members and friends. Everyone was thrilled beyond belief. It was so exciting to be sharing this milestone with them. Of course I also shared the story of Abby cheering Cam on as well. I wanted to make sure that everyone knew how proud she was. She was not yet three-years-old and yet she was able to show pride that many adults never are able to express. She sincerely was thrilled for her brother, little did she know the impact that Cameron would soon have on her world. No longer would she be able to keep her things from him because he would soon have access to everything of hers.

In December, the therapy center that Cameron attended hosts an annual holiday party for the pediatric therapy patients and their family members. It is a chance for everyone to gather and play. It is a chance to take a break from therapy and just enjoy being children. This was our first year attending the party since Cameron became a patient in January. We were so excited. Tim arranged to be off of work and the four of us attended as a family. It was an amazing party. One mom spends months getting local businesses to donate food and prizes. The therapists and staff decorate and plan games for the children. Local students volunteer to help run the games. It is truly a community effort. And of course Santa and Mrs. Claus make a guest appearance. Cameron and Abby had a blast playing games, seeing Cam's therapists and spending time with mommy and DaDa. Abby decided that she would wave to Santa but she was not going to go too close since she was afraid of Santa. Cameron decided to amaze us and everyone in the room when he let go of my hand and walked over to Santa. He was fascinated by Santa's long, white beard and glasses. Cam stood next to Santa with one hand on Santa's lap and smiled. As Tim and I watched we could not believe the confidence Cameron already had with his newly acquired walking skills. He looked like such a big boy standing by Santa!

The Best Christmas Present Ever—
The Absolute Worst Christmas!

As soon as I saw Cameron taking his first steps on December 9th I knew that I had received the best Christmas present that I could have ever hoped for. As the holiday approached I was excited. This was going to be such a different Christmas than the year before. Cam's first Christmas really was filled with so much uncertainty and so many emotions. It was overshadowed by the news that Dr. Shah had delivered in November regarding Cameron's extensive brain damage and brain atrophy. There were so many unknowns and my heart was not into celebrating. I just wanted the holiday to be over and done with. Of course we made the best of it for Abby and Cameron but Tim and I both agreed that Cam's first Christmas was the worst one we ever had. Little did we know that a worst Christmas was yet to come.

In December of 2004, as we approached Cameron's second Christmas, we enjoyed watching him taking his first steps and we happily prepared for the holiday. Tim and I enjoyed shopping for presents for the kids and wrapping the gifts. We could not wait for Christmas Eve and Christmas Day so that our family members could all see Cam walking and celebrate this milestone with us. It would be so nice to finally have a relaxing, stress free set of holidays.

Our only main concern about the holidays was Cam's food allergies. Now that Cameron was more mobile and more interested in food we knew we needed to take every precaution to keep him safe. Yes, we had a set of EpiPens in our diaper bag at all times, but our goal was to never have to use those EpiPens. We never wanted to expose Cameron to whole eggs, peanuts or tree nuts because we did not know if the EpiPen would be sufficient to help him through a life threatening reaction. Because Cameron had severe food allergies any exposure to these foods would result in an anaphylactic reaction which causes a sudden and severe drop in blood pressure and breathing difficulties. If left untreated, anaphylactic shock can lead to death within minutes. We explained the precautions that needed to be taken to all of our family members and even sent an e-mail to each explaining why we could not attend a function if these items were present. All that we asked was to be told ahead of time if someone would not be able or willing to comply with our requests so that we would not show up and have to leave abruptly. It would be sad for Abby to show up to a family function and then realize we could not stay. We did not think that our requests were unreasonable considering all that Cam had been through in his short lifetime and the fact that a life threatening situation would arise if Cameron accidentally consumed any peanuts, tree nuts or whole eggs. Of course every one of our family members said they did understand our precautions and would follow them. Again we did emphasize that we were more than willing to not attend if the precautions were too much to follow, but to let us know so that we could make alternate plans.

Imagine our surprise and extreme disappointment upon learning at 8:00 pm Christmas Eve that the house we were supposed to attend on Christmas Day was not going to follow our precautions. The message was accidentally delivered to me, by someone other than the hostess, that the hostess was planning on serving three different dishes with peanuts or tree nuts but would show us the dishes when we arrived. I was shocked. Showing me that there are life threatening foods present at a family function is irrelevant. Food could easily be dropped and Cam could easily walk up and grab something before someone could stop him. There would be no way for us to keep him safe at this house and we were not willing to endanger his life.

After I hung up the phone, I started to cry. I told Tim what I had just found out and I said that I was angry. He agreed that there was no way we would spend Christmas Day at a home that posed a threat to our son's life. Tim decided he would call and notify the hostess that we would not be able to attend if those dishes were present. When Tim called to say that he had heard that three different dishes were going to be served that contained nuts or tree nuts and if they were served then we could not attend, the hostess' response was okay, well have a nice Christmas! That was it. No, oh my gosh I am so sorry I completely forgot and I will not serve those items. Instead, she chose to tell my husband to have a nice Christmas and hung up the phone. I was so mad at this point because I was positive that she did this on purpose. This person was very jealous for the past fifteen months because of all of the "attention" we received regarding Cameron. Attention we did not want and the type of attention no parent ever wants to receive. Yes, some people did care enough to ask about Cameron and call us and offer to help us with Abby. Not this woman. This woman chose to distance herself because she was jealous. She never stopped to think about all of the painful medical procedures Cameron endured, all of the uncertainties Tim and I faced and would continue to face about our son and his future and how important celebrating this Christmas and Cam's walking milestone was to us. She only cared about herself. I was then and still am today convinced that she did this on purpose. The three dishes she chose to serve were recipes she had never made before. She found and made pumpkin bread pudding, brie cheese and a salad with pecans. The first two dishes I can guarantee you not one person attending that dinner would have eaten.

I felt and still feel like this act was a purposeful statement to how she felt about me. The sad thing was and still is is that I have known since I met this woman that she did not like me. I am not exactly sure why but that is okay with me. Neither of us would have willingly chosen to be friends with each other. I could care less if someone dislikes me so much that they do something hurtful to me. I am an adult and have realized that there will be people in this world that do not like me. But never in my life would I have expected that dislike to extend to the degree of someone being willing to put my son in a life threatening situation. He was an innocent fifteen month old little boy who had struggled with so many obstacles since birth and his life was precious. He deserved to be treated with dignity and respect and for his health and safety to never be comprised, let alone purposely compromised.

And so we spent Christmas Day at home, just the four of us. I was so upset and cried most of the day. I tried very hard to hold it together in front of Abby and Cam but then a wave of emotions would overcome me and I would break down crying. Tim was also angry and sad. The funny thing is is that when he told the hostess that we would not be able to come to dinner he did not raise his voice, sound angry or say anything inappropriate. He acted in a mature manner despite the immaturity and disrespect she showed to our family. My mom was so sad for us. She had planned to spend Christmas Day at her sister's house and invited us to come along. I declined. My aunt had not planned for us to come and so I had no idea what food she had prepared. I could not call her last minute to say we were coming and can you get rid of any unsafe foods. Plus, I was so sad that I would not have been able to hold my emotions in for the day. We stayed home and I made something that we had in the freezer. I honestly cannot even remember what it was. The hostess did not even bother to call to wish us a Merry Christmas. By evening I was feeling so upset so I grabbed my coat and went outside to take a walk all alone, on Christmas night. I walked for about forty-five minutes in the cold, dark December air. I cried and cried. I could not imagine what Tim and I had ever done that was so terrible as to warrant being treated like this. This was our time to celebrate. Our son was walking and we deserved to celebrate this great milestone. We deserved to have a great holiday. We deserved to let Cameron show everyone his new skill. And one selfish person took that away from us.

That evening, after my mom got home from my aunt's house, she called to check in on us. I broke down crying to her. I told her how I felt and how hard that this situation was. I knew that Tim and I had no choice but to keep our son away from a life threatening situation. We were responsible parents. We had and would continue to do everything we could for Cam. And yet we were being punished. We were being punished for being good parents and conscientious. I did not understand and still do not understand this. My mom cried with me. She had witnessed so many mean things that over the years this woman had done to me. And she agreed that this was certainly the topper. She told me that her whole opinion of this woman changed that day. Never again would she be able to look at her the same way. She would treat her cordially when in each other's company because my mom is a woman with dignity. This woman, however, certainly did not deserve to be treated that way, that's for sure! My mom admitted that she did not and would never have any respect for this woman who was so malicious to her daughter and daughter's family.

After I hung up with my mom, the phone rang again. This time it was my aunt. She felt terrible that we had stayed home alone for Christmas. She told me that she wished I would have called her. She would have gladly disposed of any and all unsafe foods so that we could have joined the family for Christmas. She had no idea what had happened until my mom was leaving because I made my mom promise not to say anything. My aunt cried when I told her that never in my life have I known that someone hated me enough that they would take it out on my child. After I got off of the phone with my aunt, Tim and I spoke and made the decision that we would never spend another Christmas alone. Christmas was a special holiday and we would only accept invitations for that day from people who loved our family unconditionally and would never put our son's life in jeopardy.

The hostess did not call our house to wish us a Merry Christmas or Happy New Year. And she certainly did not call to apologize for what she did. In fact it took her seventeen days, yes seventeen days, to contact us and she contacted my husband via e-mail at his work. My husband called me on January 10th to say that he had just received an e-mail from her and that he was going to forward it to me He told me he already responded back to her but wanted to see how I felt about her e-mail. I still have a copy of that e-mail and once in a while I read it. Every time I read it it makes me so angry.

In her message, she told Tim that her and her husband felt absolutely terrible about what happened with Christmas and said that she had planned on showing us the three dishes that were unsafe for Cameron when we arrived. She stated she did not think that it would be a problem since the items were not dishes that children would even want to eat. She went on to say that she and her husband wanted to meet with Tim and I to discuss what happened and any issues that we felt we had with her. She then said that she loved Abby and Cameron and deserved to be able to have a relationship with them. If any statements were true in her e-mail then she would have called back on Christmas Eve and told us that we were important to her and that she would modify her menu. She would have made contact sooner than seventeen days later and tried to rectify the situation.

I read her e-mail a few times and then Tim sent me the e-mail that he sent back to her. In it Tim held her responsible for her actions and confronted her on the fact that she knew that we would not be able to attend if she served these items and yet she chose to serve them anyway. He told her that he felt she did this on purpose because of all of the attention that Cameron and we had received since Cameron was born. He also told her that if she accidentally had chosen to make these items then when he called to say we would not be able to attend if she served the dishes she could have easily said oh I forgot and I will just throw those items out. But no, she chose to tell him oh well, have a nice Christmas and hang up. She chose not to call us on Christmas Day and apologize and try to remedy the situation by not serving those dishes. She chose to wait seventeen days to finally contact him and then it was by e-mail. And then he did the best thing he could do. He held her accountable for her actions and told her that he was angry at what she had done and that at that point he was not willing to meet and discuss the situation because he was too disappointed in her. I was so proud of Tim. He recognized that our children and their safety were more important than making amends with someone who did not take any responsibility for her actions.

And that was how we spent our son's 2nd Christmas. Yes, I can still tell you that I did receive the best Christmas present I have ever received in December of 2004. I can also tell you I had the absolute worst Christmas of my life, all thanks to a selfish person who truly will never understand the true meaning of Christmas. Recently I was talking to a good friend about whether I would include this chapter in my book or not. I said that although I think it was an important life defining moment for Tim and I where we had to choose our child's safety over attending a big holiday celebration I was afraid at the reaction that some people would have about this being publicly shared. Then I realized that I had to share this and that I could share it without indicating who the person was. If one person reads this chapter and knows someone with a life threatening food allergy it might raise awareness about the severity of it and how a family cannot take a chance by exposing their child to such a threat. And, every ounce of this chapter is true and I definitely feel the truth needs to be told! I am hoping that in the years to come the memory of this Christmas will not be so painful. I know that people say that with forgiveness comes a release of pain but I am no where near the point of forgiveness at this point. I am still angry, hurt and appalled at how this woman chose to treat our son and our family. And nothing that she has done from that point until now has shown me that I should feel any different.

The ironic part of all of this is that friends of ours make all of the accommodations that are necessary so that we can participate in birthday parties and play dates. My friend Amy will even give me all of the labels to any candy items she puts in birthday goody bags for me to double check that she has not accidentally made a mistake. It is touching to say the least that she values our friendship and my child's life that much. I now choose to spend time with people who are supportive of our family and likewise I have stepped away from those unsupportive people in my life. A wise and long overdue decision on my part! A decision that could be the basis for my next book, if I ever decide to write another book!

Abby's Turning 3!—Time for a Magical Adventure

The holidays passed and the New Year began. Tim and I talked about what a great year 2005 was going to be for us. We were excited to see the progress Cameron was making and knew that this next year was going to be a big year for him. We also marveled at Abby. She was becoming such a big girl. Her communication skills were outstanding. The things she would say to me would make me laugh so hard. She was becoming quite the little comedian. She was also approaching her 3rd birthday. On a whim in early January I looked on-line for Disney specials. I knew that Tim and I had some airline miles that would soon be expiring and I did not want to lose them. I looked to see what kind of deals we could find for hotels. I found a great rate at the Disney Pop Century, so I reserved the hotel and placed the airline tickets on hold. I waited for Tim to come home from work to run my idea past him. I wanted to take Abby to Disney World for her 3rd birthday. She deserved to have a very special birthday and I so much wanted to spend some special time with her. Tim was surprised when I told him about my idea but immediately said yes. I then needed to find out if my mom would feel comfortable watching Cameron for five days, four nights. Cameron had been doing so well physically that we felt confident that he would be okay if we went away for a few days. My mom said yes right away. I booked the trip and we were so excited.

We waited to tell Abby for a few days. Then one night we were playing mail with her. She brought over a purple plastic piece of mail to me and asked me to read it to her. I then "read" the mail to her. I told her that it said "Mommy and DaDa want to take you to Disney World for your 3rd birthday so you can meet all of the princesses." She started jumping up and down. She was so excited. She then called my mom to tell her the exciting news. She was so fascinated by all of the princesses and loved playing dress-up so we knew she would love to meet

Cinderella, Sleeping Beauty, Snow White and Belle in person. Every morning when she woke up she would ask me if we were going to Disney World that day, she just could not wait to go. A few days before we left a card arrived in the mail for Abby. She opened the card and it was a 3rd birthday card from Cinderella. In the card she found $3.00 and Cinderella wrote her a note to say that the money was for her to buy herself some suckers at Disney. She was so excited. Tim had found this special card one day and decided to send it to Abby as a surprise. She carried that card around with her until we left for our trip.

The morning of our trip my mom arrived and we went through all of Cameron's information. Abby gave Cam a big hug and kiss and we left. Cameron did not mind that we left. He was happy to spend time with my mom (we call her Me-Mom). Abby was so excited when we arrived at O'Hare airport and she saw all of the planes. We brought plenty of snacks to keep her busy during the flight and some coloring books and crayons. She made friends with a little boy and his mom that sat across the aisle from us. The flight was very smooth and right on time. Abby even fell asleep for the last half hour. She was very excited when we arrived at the Pop Century hotel. We were in the 80's section and she loved the huge can of playdoh and the giant cell phone near our room. We walked around the property and she was running in front of us saying how excited she was. Then we ate dinner. On our way back to our room we told Abby we were all going to go to sleep and the next morning she would meet the princesses. She started to cry. She told us she was ready to go home because she missed her Cameron. We told her that we would be going home in a few days and that we could call Cameron so she could talk to him. We finally convinced her to put on her princess nightgown and lay down to sleep. I can't say any of us slept well. I think Tim and I were excited to see Abby's face in the morning when she walked into Disney World, and of course all of us missed Cameron a lot.

The next morning, Wednesday, we woke early and all got ready. We took the property transportation to Disney and arrived about twenty minutes before the Magic Kingdom opened. Abby loved watching Mickey, Minnie and friends arrive in the train to open the park. We were able to take Abby on several rides during the first hour we were there. She loved the merry go round and later told us that was her favorite ride. There were no crowds and no lines for the rides so each ride we wanted to take we were able to walk right on to. Several rides she wanted to repeat and the crew would let us stay on. It was truly a magical morning. After a while Abby decided she was ready to meet her princesses. So we headed to the tent where the princesses sign autograph books. We were fortunate again to not encounter any lines. Abby was able to talk to each princess and get their autographs. We took several pictures of Abby with each princess. The smile on her face was priceless—she was so happy. She told each princess this was her birthday trip and she also told them that she had left her little brother at home with grandma. A few times during the day she would talk about Cam and how much she missed him. We called home a few times and each time Abby wanted to talk to Cameron. Cam loved listening to his sister on the phone and you could hear him laugh as we talked to him as well. My mom kept reassuring us that he was doing well and to enjoy our trip. We stayed at the park until it closed that day.

We were all so tired when we headed back to the hotel that we decided to take it easy on Thursday. We slept in and then spent the day at Downtown Disney. We then decided to head back to the Magic Kingdom on Friday. We were scheduled to fly home Saturday morning. By early evening on Thursday we were missing Cameron so much. Tim and I talked and we decided to change our plans. We were able to change our flight so we would fly home Friday night. That would work out well because we would still spend the day at the Magic Kingdom and then fly home so that Cameron would wake up to us home on Saturday. It was harder than we had imagined being away from him. We were having an absolute blast with Abby but at the same time we missed Cameron so much. And Abby was missing him terribly. She kept telling us how much she missed him.

Friday was Abby's actual 3rd birthday so when she woke up we sang Happy Birthday to her and gave her a Cinderella charm bracelet. We called home so Cameron could wish his sister a happy birthday. Then we headed to the Magic Kingdom again. Again Abby was able to go on as many rides as she wanted. She also decided to visit with the princesses again. The park was really empty and we really enjoyed it. Abby also wanted to do some shopping. She still had her money that Cinderella had sent to her and she needed to spend it. At dinner time we headed to the airport and then flew home. All three of us were tired, but a good tired. When we got home it was 11 pm and we went up to Cameron's room to see him sleeping in his crib. He must have sensed we were home because he woke up and the four of us went into our room to lie together. Abby kept hugging and kissing him. Then she also reminded him that she was now three-years-old! She told him that the next time we go to Disney we would bring him with and Tim and I readily agreed. Although he would not have enjoyed the trip being stuck in a stroller, we knew that we would never leave him again. It was so hard to be apart!

Abby talking to Cam on the phone

Therapy Changes: Physical Therapy Ends and Speech Therapy Begins

The spring brought a few changes to Cameron's therapy schedule. He had made so much progress that he no longer showed any physical delays. So the decision was made to stop physical therapy. We would continue to have physical therapy evaluations to make sure Cameron continued to meet all of his milestones on time, but we would no longer see Dolores on a regular basis. Additionally, Cameron would begin speech therapy. He really was not speaking or making any sounds and at eighteen months of age we were growing concerned. A speech evaluation did confirm our concerns. Cameron was significantly speech delayed and it was time to begin weekly speech therapy. He would continue to attend weekly occupational therapy sessions and receive monthly developmental therapy.

Cameron's schedule fit really well into our daily routine. I was able to schedule his therapies on Mondays and Tuesdays at 8 a.m. We would get home by 9:30 a.m. and then I would work from 10 am to 5 pm. I was fortunate to maintain my job despite all of Cameron's hospitalizations, doctor appointments and therapy sessions. I work for ADP, a company that prides itself on being an employer of choice and it truly is an employer of choice. I work from my home and my mom watches Abby and Cameron. My manager understands the importance of maintaining a balance between work and family. Although I miss working in the office and interacting with other associates, I feel so fortunate to be able to work from my house and work around Cameron's therapy sessions. Often times when things seemed very overwhelming I had people say well just quit your job. But I did not want to quit and could not quit. Working two days a week gave me an opportunity to focus on something other than Cameron's medical needs. Also, our medical bills were well over $1,200.00 a month and my salary allowed us to stay afloat financially. Lastly, and most importantly, I needed to work in case Tim's employment status changed. We need to maintain our health insurance due to Cameron's pre-existing condition. Since Tim and I work for the same company I know that I could obtain the same insurance for our family in case Tim was to get sick or his job was downsized. That was critical to us because we had built a team for Cameron that we were not about to change. Cameron's team consisted of Dr. Tjaden and Dr. Kaufman (Pediatricians), Dr. Nishant Shah (Neurologist), Dr. Aljadeff (Pulmonologist), Dr. Walner and Dr. Miller (ENT), Dr. Chaudwin (Allergist), Dolores (Physical Therapist), Robin (Occupational Therapist), Dana (Speech Therapist) and Jamie (Developmental Therapist). We believe that his team has played a very important part of why Cameron has done so well. Each person is committed to helping Cameron become the best that he can be. They are committed to providing our family with the emotional support that we need as well. Under no circumstances would we want to change what is working so well for Cameron and our family.

Dana worked a lot on helping Cam to improve his low muscle tone in his face and mouth so that he would be able to produce clear sounds.

Ignorance Hurts More than Cameron's Diagnosis

The spring also brought a big social change for my family and I. One of the hardest parts of having a child with special needs for me was feeling different from other moms. I was part of a playgroup with moms that I met two years earlier in a music class that Abby and I attended. Many days I felt so alone. I felt like all of the other moms that I knew had healthy children and were able to do whatever they wanted whenever they wanted. I was in a completely different situation. I could not plan ahead due to Cameron's medical issues. I could not skip Cameron's therapy sessions, specialist appointments and my two days of work. That was hard. Although our playgroup friends tried to include us in their plans we often could not attend due to these other commitments. We all tried hard though to maintain our friendship. As time passed I felt more and more like an outsider. I had changed so much since Cameron was born. I no longer felt like the same person. And to be honest I really did not know who I was, but I was not the same person that delivered Cameron a year and a half earlier. So much had happened. So many unknowns were to come. I really felt lost.

One day I learned the main reason why I no longer felt part of this group. I will be honest to write down what happened is very hard. But, it was such a key moment in our lives that I need to share it. There was one mom in the playgroup that I had grown very close to. Over the past eighteen months she was a great source of support to me. Often times I would call her and cry and she would listen. She seemed to care—she really did. I have to say that I have never misjudged someone's character more than I did of this woman. For a few weeks I was feeling like something was amiss with our friendship. There was something bothering me and I could not pinpoint what it was. Then one day I discovered exactly what it was. We were talking on the phone and she interrupted me and said I have something I need to tell you. I said "Okay, well tell me." Here is what she said word for word...."You know I love Cameron, but I would never want to have a Cameron. I would never want to be a parent of a child with special needs." I was stunned. I actually did not know what to say. At that moment Cameron was crying so I said I needed to go and I would talk to her later. I hung up the phone and cried. I could not believe how cruel she could be. I did not understand how she could say what she said let alone feel what she felt. I just could not believe it. I did not answer the phone when she called later that day. I actually did not answer the phone at all that day. I did not want to talk to anyone. I stayed in the house with the kids. Tim came home from work and he could tell something was wrong but I did not tell him what had happened. That night I tossed and turned. I could not forget what this mom had said. I cried. I did not feel that way at all about Cameron. I honestly could not imagine our lives without him and I would not change him. He was such a gift and I felt blessed. I knew what I needed to do. I needed to end this friendship. The problem was that this group was a clique in every sense of the word. If I told this mom I was no longer interested in a friendship with her then it would mean that I would be isolated from this group. The thought of walking away from the playgroup I was part of for two years was scary. I was so afraid to start over. And yet I had no choice. In my heart I knew that I needed to walk away. I would rather have no friends than to have a friend (and possibly a group of friends) who could not see what a joy our son was in our life. I also thought about Abby. How would she feel if she ever heard someone say something so absolutely cruel about her brother? She loved Cameron with all of her heart. She might have only been three-years-old but she was so much wiser than this woman was and many adults are. She knew that every person's life deserves to be celebrated.

The next day this woman called and we started to talk. I had nothing to say and never would. I could tell her about all of the joy Tim and I feel in our lives due to both of our children. I could tell her how much more fulfilling our lives were now that Cameron joined us. But for what? She was ignorant and I am sorry to say she always will be. I am more than happy to share all of the joy that Cameron brings into our lives with others. I want to support other parents as they begin their journey into the world of therapies, medical specialists, and special-needs parenting. I want to tell others that your life will never be the same but it truly will be better than you could have ever imagined if you open your heart and embrace your child. Although it might not be easy to balance the needs of your child with special needs, the love and joy this child will bring to your life will outweigh those difficulties. I chose to end this friendship with my dignity intact. I told this woman that our lives were so different now and with all of Cameron's appointments I had decided not to get together with her or the playgroup. And again this woman showed her true self to me. Before I could finish my sentence she interrupted me and said "Oh, so what are you going to do—only hang out with people who have children with special needs now?" I said no, I am going to spend some time enjoying my children. She hung up on me. Later that day I called the other two women in the playgroup and thanked them for all of their support and told them we would no longer be joining them for play dates. Again I just said that our lives were so different now and I needed to spend some time alone with Abby and Cameron. They already knew because the other woman had called them and already spread the news.

I did not sleep well again. In the middle of the night Tim realized I was up and he asked what was wrong. I told him all that had happened. He told me that he was so proud of me because I had put our family first. He also told me that he considered Cameron to be a blessing and never would he allow someone to say anything but that. Then I told him that the biggest fear I had when I heard that Cameron might have cerebral palsy had come true. I always worried that someone would make fun of him or exclude him because he might be different—maybe he would walk differently, talk differently, etc. I also worried how much that might hurt Abby in addition to him. My biggest fear had come true but rather than from a child I heard this from another mom. She did not want to have a child with special needs. She would not want to have our son as her own son. How could anyone be so cruel? I told Tim if this is how an adult is willing to act then what would the future be like in terms of other children. If children are being raised by parents that do not accept disabilities then how would they ever learn to accept them?

I felt relieved to have ended these friendships. I needed to spend time with Abby and Cameron, enjoying them, playing with them and most of all teaching them what the meaning of unconditional love was through example. It would have been hypocritical for me to maintain any type of relationship with this woman. As the week went on I started to feel better. I felt at peace with my decision and it was time to move on. Imagine my surprise when I arrived home on Good Friday to find my porch loaded with everything and anything I ever gave or loaned these three women and their children. Collectively they decided it would be a good idea to leave everything on my porch for me to find. As I drove up and realized what I was seeing I started to cry. I could not believe how incredibly mean people could be. I sat in the garage and sobbed. Abby kept asking me if I was okay and I tried to stop crying but I could not. I have to say that this experience was harder than finding out our son had cerebral palsy. I felt so angry at our circumstances. I loved this little boy with all of my heart and I wanted everyone else to as well. And I learned that there are people in this world filled with intolerance for differences. I actually hit the lowest point of my life that day. I called Tim at work to tell him what happened. He could not even believe it. He had had it with these women. He said they definitely crossed the line. He wanted to go to each of their homes and confront them but we both knew that was not the answer.

And so together we grieved. We grieved for our son and daughter and the fact that they would grow up in a society filled with people not accepting of differences. And we decided that we could do one of two things—we could let these women and their ignorance consume us or we could move forward. We chose to move forward. Rather than isolate ourselves from the world we would just be more cautious of the friends we made. We decided that the quantity of friends that one has is irrelevant but the quality of a friend is of utmost importance. I spent the summer with my children. We played in our yard, we took long walks, we laughed, we talked and we enjoyed some peaceful times. I avoided this group of women. I knew that if I ran into one of them, let alone the group, that I would be an emotional wreck. I needed my distance because I needed time to heal. And I needed to stop giving their ignorance power in our lives. The anger I felt was so all consuming. Never in my life has something angered me more. Over time the anger has diminished. I wish I could say it is gone but it is not. And I wish I could say that these women do not bother me, but that is not the case either. I still occasionally run into the one woman and I still cannot bear to look her in her eyes or speak to her. She attempted to talk to me a few months back and I walked right by her. I will never again listen to any words she has to speak. I will never again give her an opportunity to hurt me like she has.

And so this experience has changed us. I know what is important in my life and that is my children, both of my children. They are both so different and so equally loved. They are both so wanted and such a blessing. I truly cannot imagine my life without both of them. I am blessed, that I know!

I talked to Dolores, Cameron's physical therapist, about what happened with the playgroup women. She was outraged. She was sad. But most of all she was concerned that I would isolate Abby and Cameron from everyone. Even though we had been hurt she stressed the importance of meeting other families and Abby and Cameron meeting friends. I agreed with her. I was scared but yet I did know that we needed to take a chance and let people into our lives or else we would all suffer. I told her of my fears of someday Abby realizing that someone might be making fun of Cameron for something he had no control over. She said all of my fears were fears that she had heard other moms express to her. She also told me of an upcoming seminar that she thought might be beneficial to both Tim and I. The seminar was titled "Understanding the Needs of Siblings of Children with Special Needs." The speaker, Dr. Richard Ney, was a father of a son with autism, and he would be presenting along with his daughter, Liz. Tim and I decided to attend. It was a beneficial seminar. Liz shared experiences with the audience of growing up with a brother with special needs. She spoke of times when he was excluded and how that made her feel and what her parents did to help her through those times. She also shared with us that she was studying to become an occupational therapist. We learned that evening that a high percentage of siblings of children with special needs enter professions working with children with special needs. Many become special education teachers, physical therapists, occupational therapists and speech therapists.

Dr. Ney asked the audience if they had questions and I decided to share what had happened with this group of women and see if his family had experienced anything similar and to see if he could offer any words of wisdom. After I explained what had happened he said sadly they also had encountered situations such as that and had made similar choices to do what we had done. Then he went on to say something that I never will forget. Dr. Ney said "You did not become a parent of a child with special needs by accident. God chose you and your husband to be your son's parents." How powerful is that statement? I sat there and thought about what he just said. And I firmly believed it was true. Not only did we love our son unconditionally, but we were willing to get him every ounce of help he needed. We were willing to be completely unselfish and put his needs above our own. He deserved to be the best he could be and we were committed to making sure he was given all of the interventions he needed to succeed. Not everyone would do that.

As Tim and I drove home we talked about the seminar. Both of us felt it was very beneficial. I then asked Tim what was the most important thing he learned that night. He told me that God chose us to be Cameron's parents—it was not an accident. I agreed. Many times since Cameron got sick I questioned God. I wondered why God would allow Cameron to get so sick, allow Cameron to have brain damage, present Cameron with so many obstacles. And I realized that God knew that Cameron would have parents who would walk with him through his journey, side by side, hand in hand. He chose us for this important role and he knew that Cameron would be a fighter. God knew that through Cameron's journey Cam would touch the lives of so many people. I thank God every day that he saw the strength in us that we might have never imagined we would have.

Selecting a Preschool for Abby

One of the most important decisions that we made for Abby ended up being one of the best decisions we made for our entire family. In the winter of 2005 just before I chose to leave the playgroup we made an important decision about preschool. Abby had just turned three and she would be able to start preschool in the upcoming fall. We are lucky to live in an area that offers many different choices of preschool programs. There are park district preschools, preschools with a religious affiliation and public preschools. I felt a bit overwhelmed when the topic of preschool arose in our playgroup. Two of the three moms were former school teachers and had very strong but opposing views on what to look for in a preschool. The other mom had a friend who told her all about the best preschool program around and it was called TLC preschool located at Trinity Lutheran Church in downtown Huntley. She had her daughter on a waiting list for the program since her daughter was two months old. I had placed Abby's name on the waiting list when she was one-and-a-half-years-old along with the other playgroup moms when she told us about the program. Of course as spring arose each of these moms were called because their child's name was up on the waiting list. So the one mom who convinced all of us that this was the best preschool went to tour the program with her daughter. This mom decided that this was not the program for her daughter and so the other two moms decided the same thing. It was actually funny because each child in the playgroup was so different and yet eventually these three moms would choose the identical preschool program for their children. TLC did not call me. I called to see where Abby was on the list but she was still about twenty names down on the list. It did not seem like she would be able to get in. I did ask the director to keep us on the list though. I started to take Abby to the various programs in the area. One thing I knew that I did not want was a program where you drive up and drop your child off at the curb side and the teacher then takes the child in. I wanted to bring Abby to her classroom each day and pick her up. That was important to me. I also knew that this was going to be a big transition for Abby. And I wanted her to feel comfortable with me leaving. Even though I had Cameron and he was very active and it might be challenging getting him to stay with Abby and I in the school hallway, we were going to do this as a family. Abby and I both liked the park district program so I received the enrollment forms to fill out. I had decided that this program would be a good fit for Abby. I also learned that the other moms chose another program where you drive up and drop your child off curbside. It was funny because the one mom said this was something she did not want, but I guess the thought of choosing something that was best for her child was not as important to her as following the clique and selecting the program the other moms would be joining. It was also funny because within three hours of one mom visiting this program all three moms had signed their children up and had called me to tell me to go right over and sign Abby up since there were only two remaining morning spots. I told them that I was not interested in that program due to the curbside drop off. They were shocked because of course this was the best preschool in the area since their children would all be attending it. I did not budge. I was not interested and actually was happy that they chose what they did and I did not let them influence my decision.

Needless to say I was thrilled when just after Abby's birthday, Mrs. Hansen, the director of the TLC preschool called to say that Abby's name had reached the top of the waiting list and wanted to know if we were still interested in their program. I was interested and we set up an appointment for Abby and I to visit. When we arrived at TLC for our appointment Abby and I were both impressed. You could feel the love and the presence of the children throughout the building. Beautiful artwork adorned the hallways, backpacks hung on hooks and there was laughter in the air. And then we were greeted by Mrs. Hansen. Her smile was contagious. She was the director and founder of TLC. This was not a job to her, rather it was her passion. Abby quickly grabbed Mrs. Hansen's hand as we walked through the school. When we entered one of the classrooms I watched as Abby looked around the room. The teacher and teacher's assistant introduced themselves to Abby and asked Abby her name. And Abby spoke to them. She looked at ease and comfortable. She was not shy at all. They let her play with some of the children in the water table and I was able to observe the happenings in the classroom. I loved it. And Abby loved it. She was happy. I ended up writing a check for Abby's registration fee and getting the paperwork to fill out for her enrollment. We found Abby's preschool. She was so excited. We learned that there would be a toy washing day in August so the children could meet their teachers and classmates as well as help get the toys ready for the school year. We learned that every other week there would be a new theme that would be incorporated into the lesson plan such as confidence and believing in yourself, helping and being a good friend, thankfulness, patience and generosity and tolerance and acceptance, to name a few. We talked about holiday celebrations. All Christian holidays would be celebrated. In fall we would celebrate Noah's Ark day instead of Halloween. Each child would dress up as an animal and the children would learn all about Noah's Ark. They would also have a special Christmas program. I was so excited. I could not wait to get home and read the parent handbook and tell Tim all about the program. Abby called my mom (Me-Mom) to tell her that she would be attending TLC.

Throughout the summer Abby talked excitedly about starting preschool in the fall. She would pretend she was a teacher and Cameron was one of the students in her class and she would read stories to him. We talked about preschool and what Abby's teachers' names were. We also talked about how mommy and Cam would be dropping her off and picking her back up after school. She seemed very excited and never let on to me that she was nervous about me leaving. Her first day of school at TLC was called Easy Start. Half of her class would be there and parents stay as well. It gives everyone a chance to meet the teacher and learn what their days at school are going to be like. Tim was able to take the day off of work so that we could both take Abby to Easy Start. Cameron would stay home so that we could give Abby 100% of our attention. She woke up that morning to a big Strawberry Shortcake balloon and a special card from Tim and I. She was thrilled. We took over fifty pictures—of her brushing her teeth, with her backpack on, with Cameron and then at school. She really was excited and did very well at school. They took a picture of us with Abby so that they would have a picture to hang in her classroom for her to always see. It really was a fun day and we were even more excited for school to start.

On Abby's first day of school my mom came over to watch Cameron. Again Abby was excited but she did seem a little nervous too. I told her that I would be dropping her at school and then after school I would be back for her. My mom told me to take the morning to myself and that she would watch Cameron. I took Abby to school and we were early. She washed her hands and hung up her backpack and then we sat in the hallway and watched as the other preschoolers arrived. Abby was starting to get nervous and decided to sit on my lap. We really did not know any of the other children or families yet so we just sat and waited for Abby's teacher, Mrs. Werber, to open the classroom door. Mrs. Werber was a new teacher to TLC but was a seasoned preschool teacher. She had run an at home preschool for many years and was very knowledgeable about early education. When she opened the door for class to start Abby started to cry a little. Mrs. Werber asked all of the parents to walk their child to the door, give them a hug and then to leave. From experience she knew that it is better to say good-bye and leave than to hover and prolong the good-byes. Abby cried as she walked into the room and I cried as I walked to my car. I felt so torn. I knew she was going to have a wonderful time at school and I knew her teachers were very loving and caring women, but I hated to see her sad about me leaving. I tried to run a few errands to keep my mind off of leaving Abby and then at 11 am I went back to TLC to wait for Abby's class to end. I sat there with another mom, Beth, who I would become very good friends with as the year continued. Beth's daughter Gracie was also a little weepy when she went into class and so Beth also returned a little early so that she was sure she would be right there when class ended. We chatted a little while we both waited to see our daughters. When class ended and Mrs. Werber excused each student one by one Abby came running out of her classroom with a big smile and a huge hug for me. She told me all about what a fun day she had.

Our TLC Preschooler!

Since Abby was in the three-year-old preschool program she would be attending school on Thursdays and Fridays. On Friday my mom watched Cameron again so I could take Abby to school. Again Abby cried right before entering the classroom but had another great day. Since she then had a few days off before her next day of class Abby was nervous when we went to school the second week. I took Cameron with. I decided we needed to start our normal routine which would include Cameron helping to bring his sister to school and pick her up. I did put Cam in the stroller when we walked into school because I did not want him roaming the halls freely. Plus the hallway was quite narrow and I knew if he escaped from me I would have a hard time catching up to him with all of the parents and preschoolers around. When it was time for Abby to go into her classroom she really started to cry. I did not know what to do but Mrs. Werber took her hand and brought her into her room. She was crying so hard and I felt terrible. After she closed the door I started to cry and walked down to the director's office to talk to her. Mrs. Hansen was so supportive and understanding. She told me that every year she does have a few parents who also cry and handed me the box of Kleenex. She assured me that I was doing the right thing by letting her go into the room without me and that some children take longer to adjust to preschool than others do. She was aware of all that our family had been through the past two years with Cameron's health and she did feel that might be playing a part in Abby's apprehensiveness about leaving me. I told her that I wondered if I was to blame for Abby's insecurity. During Cameron's first year of life there were so many times that I was gone unexpectedly to the hospital with Cam. I wondered if Abby lost her ability to trust that I really would come back to her because I had chosen to be with Cameron at the hospital. I always felt guilty about that. I had two children to take care of and sometimes I had to put Cameron first when he was in the hospital because I could not be in two places at once. Logically I know what I did was the right thing for our family at the time, but nonetheless as a mom I still feel guilty about my decision. After I talked to Mrs. Hansen I did feel much better. After that day, Abby did fine when I would drop her at school. I would reassure her that I would be picking her back up and Cam and I always made sure we got back early.

Cameron, however, missed his sister. For the first few weeks he would look for Abby after we would leave school. I would take him to various parks and for walks because I wanted to avoid doing errands during our alone time. He did enjoy his time with mommy but he was always looking for Abby. Cameron loved seeing all of the other moms and he waited for Abby to run out of her class to see him. Each time she came out of class she would shower Cam with lots of hugs and kisses. It was so cute. You would have thought they had not seen each other for months the way she would greet him.

Cameron grew tired of sitting in the stroller and within a few weeks I started to let him walk into school with us. It was so challenging. He did not want to sit and wait in the hallway for Abby to go into her class or at the end to come out. Many days he would run into the girls' bathroom and touch the potties. Abby thought it was fun but I found it to be quite stressful. The hallway was crowded and it was hard to keep an eye on Cameron. He was quite the mischievous little boy. He loved to peek into Abby's room at the end of the day too. Sometimes Mrs. Werber would see him looking in and invite us in for the last few minutes of class. He loved that and so did Abby. The day usually ended with the children singing a song or listening to a song on the cd player so Cameron was excited to participate.

We met so many nice families at TLC and started to have play dates with children in Abby's class as well as the other classes. All of the children got along very well and it was fun for the moms to get to know each other better. I found myself opening up to meeting new people and forming friendships again. It was such an easy thing to do because the moms I met were very caring people who I enjoyed getting to know.

Cameron Turns 2!

Cameron turning two was not as emotional as when he turned one. I think that knowing that we had his diagnosis already made this birthday easier. Plus Cam was doing so very well. He was really amazing in terms of his physical abilities and we were again feeling more confident about his health. We decided to have a very small birthday party this year. We would invite just our parents and our siblings and their families. Although we were excited to be celebrating his second birthday we really had not had a big birthday party for Abby's second so we felt we should celebrate in a small way for Cam's second birthday as well. We did choose a safari party theme because Cameron really was showing so much interest in jungle animals. I decided to make his birthday invitations using a new monkey stamp set that I purchased. Cam was our little monkey so it only seemed fitting to have monkey invitations. Before his birthday party we went and had his professional birthday pictures taken in a safari looking outfit with a hat that I had chosen. He looked adorable. And he looked so grown up. I could not believe when I got his pictures back how much he now looked like a toddler and less like a little baby. He was getting a bit taller and was quite lean looking—no baby chunkiness left to him at all. Of course that did not surprise us due to his high energy level.

We're all ready for my 2nd birthday party!

I also wrote Cameron the following birthday letter:

Cameron,

When I think about this last year all that I can say is WOW! You are an amazing little boy Cameron! This past year has been filled with so many big milestones for you. At the time of your first birthday you were mastering crawling and really enjoying your new found freedom. You enjoyed crawling after Abby to see what she was doing and you especially liked playing with toys that she left behind as she moved on to her next toy. You also were able to stand up provided you were holding on to something.

Well, shortly after your first birthday you decided you did not want to only crawl. You wanted to be able to move quicker. So, you ventured out and began to cruise along furniture and walk using your walking toy. You were excited to be gaining more independence and loved when we would clap for you. You felt so much pride. In November I really wanted to purchase your first pair of walking shoes so we went to Stride Rite one Sunday afternoon with Abby and DaDa. You were tired and you fell asleep in your stroller and did not wake up while the girl measured your foot size and put your new shoes on you. It was so funny. DaDa of course took pictures of this! Mommy picked a white leather pair of shoes with little blue dinosaurs on the back. They were adorable. We woke you up once you had them on and you looked down at your feet and smiled. I guess you knew that you would need these very soon!

On December 9th you gave mommy the best Christmas present I could have ever wished for—you walked—all by yourself! You were in your physical therapy session alone and Abby and I came in to join you for the final few minutes. As we walked in we stopped and just watched—you were walking all by yourself across the entire therapy center—over 30 steps. I started to cry. Abby started to cheer you on—she was so proud of you. Of course you loved our attention. Abby then ran over to give you a big hug and you fell on your butt—the two of you started laughing so hard and of course that made mommy cry even more. I cannot describe to you the joy I felt watching you take those first steps Cameron. You looked so confident and so big to me. And you were so proud. I called DaDa at work to tell him and he actually started to cry on the phone—this was a moment we had waited and hoped for … it was truly one of the happiest days of my life. It was so much fun to watch Abby cheering you on—little did she know the impact you were now going to have on her world—nothing would stop you now!

Another big milestone you accomplished this year was running. You decided shortly after you started to walk that it was time to run. And boy are you fast. I have to chase you all around the house when I want to change your diaper, dress you or give you a bath. You laugh so hard and it is so funny. It is also so tiring! At the end of the day I collapse into bed—but it truly is the best tired feeling I have ever felt.

You are also now our climber. Up until now you did not try to climb on anything—I think because you were so small in height. Well you have decided that regardless of how tall you are that you are going to climb on everything that you want. I have found you at the top of the stairs, on the back of the couch and on top of the kitchen table! You have no fear! And one of the cutest climbing moments is when we have the refrigerator open and you climb in to stand in the fridge and drink your BaBa.

Another special moment that sticks in my mind is hearing your beautiful voice call me DaDa. This year you have started to say a few words. You can say hi, bye, DaDa and BaBa. Well recently you say Hi DaDa. So whenever you see me you say Hi DaDa. Of course I laugh and when I tell you no—I am MaMa—you call me DaDa more—and you laugh. I know you know that I am your mommy but you insist on calling me dada. I can't wait to hear you say mama or mommy.

For your birthday we decided to have a monkey/safari theme since you are such our little monkey. Mommy made special monkey invitations and we even bought a large inflatable monkey. You laughed when you saw it. I also made cupcakes with animal figures on each. You smiled when you saw them but you would not even try a bite—you are still not very interested in eating … I am sure that will change someday soon.

Happy 2nd Birthday Cam! Thank you for filling my heart with so much joy again this past year. I cannot even imagine what changes this next year will bring! I am sure you have a lot of wonderful surprises in store for all of us.

I love you with all of my heart,
Mommy

Time to Move!

In October of 2005, when Cameron was just over two we began to receive information about Cameron's transition from Early Intervention to the school district. We learned that once a child reaches the age of three they are no longer eligible to receive services through Early Intervention. Each school district is legally obligated to provide services to children over the age of three who are deemed at risk. Due to Cameron's diagnosis of cerebral palsy as well as his developmental delays he would qualify to attend our school district's at risk preschool program. Our Early Intervention office hosts an annual information meeting about the transition process so parents understand what to expect in terms of the transition process. Rather than working under the guidelines of an IFSP (Individual Family Service Plan) when Cameron turned three and entered the school system we would begin to work under the guidelines of an IEP (Individualized Education Plan). We would have paperwork to fill out for the school system and Cameron would undergo evaluations so that as a group the school district representatives, as well as Tim and I, could create an IEP to guide Cameron's educational services on a yearly basis. There are laws that define the IEP process and the services that Cameron is entitled to receive.

The thought of Cameron turning three and transitioning to the school district was scary. Although it was still eleven months away I was worried. We had worked hard the past year and a half to create a therapy plan that was working so well for Cameron. Cameron had a therapy team that he had been with from the start. Although he no longer saw Dolores for physical therapy sessions she still followed him for evaluations. He was thriving in his weekly occupational therapy sessions with Robin and loving working on his communication skills during his speech therapy session with Dana. And monthly Cam enjoyed seeing Jamie for his developmental therapy work. We all knew one another very well and I felt 100% confident that Cameron was receiving the most loving care possible. He was thriving and so incredibly happy. But before long Cam's entire team was about to change. We would have to depend on people we did not know to capture Cameron's heart and spirit and inspire him to continue to thrive in an entirely different environment. That is a huge responsibility to ask of others.

Tim and I were very nervous about the school district we lived in. Although we had carefully chosen our home six years earlier and had checked on the school district at that time and had learned it was a great district, a lot had changed in the six years. The area we lived in was experiencing an enormous amount of growth and the school district was trying hard to keep up with the large influx of new students. In the past year there were many negative feelings in the community regarding the school district. A proposed tax referendum had passed for some much needed funding to help our district keep up with the growth to only later be discovered that there were many erroneous facts that were presented to home owners by certain school officials as a way to have the referendum pass. Additionally, the proposed tax amount that home owners were promised was also not true. There were daily articles in the paper from angry home owners and a division of loyalty amongst members of the school district board. Resignations by the superintendent and CFO followed. And the manner in which home owners were persuaded to vote yes for the referendum angered people. There were many "threats" that if the referendum did not pass then school hours were going to be changed and many programs would be eliminated or scaled down. It really gave many home owners (a.k.a. tax payers) a negative impression of the district.

After I attended the transition meeting at our Early Intervention office in October of 2005 we would make a drastic life change. Prior to the meeting all parents were asked to RSVP. Due to not having a babysitter, Tim and I decided that I would attend this information meeting alone. On the RSVP forms you were asked to indicate what school district you resided in because representatives would be attending from each school district to also answer questions and provide information packets about their program. The overall meeting was very informative and helpful. There was a discussion on what an IEP was and how the IEP process works. There was a presentation by Angela, one of the parent liaisons, about the transition from a parent perspective and about the concerns that parents have. Angela provided us with some helpful tips. And there were other presentations as well. After the formal presentations we were told to go to certain areas of the building to meet with the representatives from our specific school district. I walked around and located the representative for our school district.

The next hour would impact our lives drastically. As I stood near our school district area I was surprised to see how many parents were gathering in the area. I knew that our district had a lot of students and that growth was an issue but I did not ever stop to think about how that would impact our family in terms of the at risk preschool program. Approximately twenty-five families were represented at this meeting. I was immediately put off when the school district representative mentioned she did not bring enough materials for everyone. I can understand being under by a few but she brought a total of seven packets of information and she had not even bothered to put the packets together. So she was trying to quickly put the packets together and we all realized that she did not bring enough materials. I was angry that she was not prepared for such an important meeting for our families. For many of us this was our first encounter with the school district and to be honest it left a terrible first impression. All of our families had RSVP'd that we would be attending this meeting therefore this representative knew how many families would be there and yet she did not bother to take the time to prepare the necessary materials for each of us. I was disappointed. But this would not be nearly as disappointing as what happened next.

After the representative spoke briefly about the process and the district's program, a mom standing next to me asked an excellent question. Her son would be turning three in February and she wondered what happened when a child turned three in the middle of the school year and how the teachers handle making a child feel part of a group that has been together for several months. What I would hear next shocked me, angered me and made me make a big financial decision for our family. The school representative told this mom that most likely her son would not be entering the program at that point because it would be filled. The mom explained that her son had been in Early Intervention since birth and had never had a break in his therapy so if the program was full then he would have a break in services for over seven months. The school representative then said that legally the district did not have to worry about this because a school district has nine months to provide services to a child who ages out of Early Intervention. Furthermore, it would have been better if her son would have been born in August or September, since there are always open spaces at the beginning of a school year. With that she looked around and asked if anyone else had questions. I looked at this mom and she said I can't believe this—I don't know what we will do. We talked a bit and we both said how absolutely unimpressed we were with the school district already.

When I got home Tim asked all about the evening. I told him all about it and then told him about this family whose son is turning three in February and what the representative told the mom. He was shocked. I was so angry. I told him we were going to check further into our school district and others to decide where Cameron would attend school and ultimately Abby too. Tim was confused and he said they have to attend in the district in which you live. Of course I knew that. I told him well we might be moving. He just looked at me.

The next day I began my research of the school district and surrounding districts. I began speaking to other parents of children with special needs including Angela, the parent liaison of EI, Cameron's therapists and Abby's preschool director. I learned that Crystal Lake, Illinois has a wonderful special education program and many parents relocate to Crystal Lake for the preschool program for children who are at risk. I also found out that many of the staff members have long tenure with the district and the district has little turn over. I decided after about two weeks of inquiry that we would be moving to Crystal Lake. Tim was not so easily convinced. I began scouring realtor.com and looking at various real estate agent's Web sites of homes for sale. I also began driving around and decided based on parental input that I wanted to live in the Woodscreek Subdivision. Over 80% of students in Woodscreek walk to school which was another important factor to us. I wanted to make sure our children could be walked to school rather than rely on a bus due to many factors, including Cameron's severe food allergies which require him to have a qualified person with him that would know how to administer an EpiPen. Bus drivers are not trained to administer an EpiPen and although we are told no food is allowed on the school bus we know that the potential does exist that children might bring food and share food during the bus ride. Cameron's egg, peanut and tree nut allergies are so severe that every second will matter if he has a severe reaction. I decided to contact Sharon Gidley, a realtor that a few of our family members had previously worked with to start showing us homes. She took us to some homes in Woodscreek and we fell in love with one home. It was a corner lot and exactly two blocks from school. It was a four bedroom three and a half bath home and it had a finished basement. We would be moving out of our home that we had built and loved—we had a three bedroom two and a half bath brick front two story home with a full front porch, finished basement, beautiful fenced lawn and we lived six doors down from my mom. We knew we did not want to downsize due to the kids and all of their toys. We also knew as time went on we would continue to accumulate things so we wanted to have more space rather than less. We also still wanted to be in the area. This new home was exactly three miles from our current home. It was listed at $339,000, which was a bit higher than what we were willing to pay. We knew whatever home we bought we would be putting in new carpet and flooring since Cameron's asthma and allergies were so severe. We also knew it would cost us to hire movers and to redecorate a new home. So we asked Sharon to make an offer of $315,000. We were willing to make the offer non-contingent. It was scary to do that because we were risking being double owners and we were entering the holiday season. The home owners rejected our offer and so Tim and I decided we would start looking for another home. We knew we would find something, however, there were not many homes currently for sale in the Woodscreek subdivision. We wanted to move quickly. We knew that Cameron's transition paperwork would begin six months before he turned three, which would mean March. We also knew that in the spring our taxes were going to increase substantially on our house due to the tax referendum that had passed for our current school district and we worried that the increase might make our home harder to sell. We needed to sell our home and sell it quickly. Tim was leaving for a business trip so we agreed to look again when he returned. Meanwhile Sharon wanted to list our current home but we said no. Although we were scared to be double owners, we were more fearful of selling our home and not having another home to move into. Our house had a lot of curb appeal, since only two homes in our neighborhood had the elevation we chose and our house was in pristine condition. It was probable that our home would sell very quickly. As luck would have it the offer we originally made ended up being accepted by the other home owners. They were getting desperate to sell because they were double owners and needed to sell even if they were getting a lot less than their asking price. Tim was thrilled when I called to tell him and we set a closing date for December 15th. Sharon would come by the following morning to get our house listed. I put the kids to bed and spent the entire evening organizing my cabinets, closets and the toys. Although our house was very clean and organized, I still felt like I needed to clean it more. It might have been because I was nervous. We were making a big decision and financially I was worried. Yes, we could afford to own both homes for a few months, but not indefinitely. It was November. The holidays were coming and the real estate market was slow. Nonetheless I knew that we were doing the right thing. Since our current home was only three bedrooms we listed it for $289,000. We had immediate results. We had several showings and a signed contract within five days of our listing for $280,000. We were so excited. That contract would fall through, however. The couple buying our home had a home inspection done and there were only a few items the inspector found and they decided to pursue. The furnace needed to be cleaned and they wanted a surface crack repaired in the basement. Also, they wanted confirmation that the outlets in the kitchen were GFI outlets. That was a joke. The buyers had paid $300.00 for a professional home inspection and their inspector did not even know that the outlets in the kitchen were indeed GFI outlets. Our home was only six-years-old and it was code in our village like most that outlets in a kitchen are GFI. We laughed. The buyers also wanted the Rainbow Play System swing set removed from our yard even though it was under one-year-old, one of the best brand swing sets you could buy in our area and they had a small child. We had our attorney tell the buyers we would agree to have the basement crack sealed and have the swing set removed but we would not pay for the furnace to be cleaned. Cleaning a furnace is considered standard maintenance and our furnace had been professionally cleaned less than six months earlier. These buyers seemed difficult to us because they also wanted us to close on the house in less than three weeks. We agreed though because we were scared and did not want to turn away a buyer. Well, the furnace cleaning became a deal breaker. The buyer's realtor was a very pushy lady and told our realtor if we did not have the furnace cleaned it would be a deal breaker. I was so upset and told Tim that based on the principle of this in terms of how we were being treated with their demands, three week closing time, and swing set removal that we were not budging. We were not going to do a maintenance item. The buyers must have thought we would be afraid by their threat and when we did not back down they let the contract rescind. We were relieved because we started to worry that we would find ourselves having to give in to other demands at closing. We were scared but honestly more relieved. We also did not want to sell our home to people who would turn out to be bad neighbors since my mom lived only six houses away. We recently learned this couple separated and divorced. After they signed our house contract they decided they were not going through with the purchase and rather than being truthful to us they caused us an enormous amount of distress by pushing us into backing out of the contract. A lot more can be said about this situation and what transpired between our realtor and the buyers' realtor, but suffice it to say that we chose the higher ground and walked away.

Our house went back on the market the week of Thanksgiving and sold in three days. The new buyers wanted to be in the house by Christmas and we set a closing date of December 15th. We moved up our closing on our new house to December 1st. We needed to have a few weeks overlap to have all of our work done on our new house before we could move in. We scheduled painting, new carpet, flooring, appliances, plumbing work, new countertops and sink in the kitchen and a bunch of electrical work. Everything was proceeding as planned. But, the contract on our house fell through again. I was devastated and angry. How could this be happening to us? We were doing this for all of the right reasons and yet nothing seemed easy. Tim and I never got a break. It seemed like no matter what we did we ran into problems. This second set of buyers lost their buyer due to a mold issue and they were not willing to buy our home without a contingency. I was so upset. And so frightened. We had moved up our closing date and had started all of our work on our new home. We were spending all of this money and now we had no buyer. And Christmas was quickly approaching. Plus we knew that an unfurnished home does not sell as well as a furnished home, so we would not be moving into our new house until our current home sold. It was such a sad situation. Luckily, after a few very tense days the buyers decided to proceed with no contingency and wanted the closing date to be December 23rd. Tim and I said that was a great Christmas present. On December 22nd we moved into our new house. It was a lot more work to move than we ever anticipated. My mom helped a lot by watching Abby and Cameron many evenings so Tim and I could move things to the new house and clean. And thankfully we did hire movers for all of the big items.

Abby seemed excited about the move. She would continue to attend her same preschool program and our new house had a Rainbow Play System swing set that was twice the size of our old one. We also let her decide how to decorate her room. She decided she wanted her room to be pink and light purple with a white chair rail. And she wanted wood flooring in her bedroom like Cameron. We created a beautiful princess room for her. We also decided to create a jungle theme room for Cam. Cam loves animals and so we had his room painted a medium taupe color and we hung a jungle theme border. It turned out great and he really liked his room.

December 21st was our first night in our new house and it was rough. We slept on the floor in our bedroom while we waited for our movers to move our furniture in on December 22nd. No one slept well. We were all excited. And Tim and I were a bit nervous too. We hoped the weather would cooperate especially since it was December in the Chicago area and we knew a bad snow storm could hit at any moment. We also were hoping that nothing would happen with our closing on the 23rd. We wanted to be done with our house sale. We went to bed late on December 22nd. We had unpacked so much stuff already. We set up the entire basement with all of the kids' toys and their rooms were all together. We still had some boxes to unpack and a lot of items to hang up, but we were in our new home and had all of our necessities unpacked. The closing on the 23rd went perfectly and the buyers of our old home were happy. We were so relieved. We wanted the kids to have a special Christmas despite our move, so we put our Christmas tree up at our new house and even hosted Christmas Eve. I was exhausted and so was Tim. But 2005 ended with us being owners of only one home and a home in the school district we wanted to be in. We knew that 2006 was going to be a great year!

Home Therapy—Challenges it Brings—Standing up for Cameron

Cameron started receiving therapy at just four months of age. After his initial evaluation by Early Intervention we were able to receive an HMO referral to obtain physical therapy at a therapy center a few miles from our house. Since I only had Abby who was twenty-three months at the time and Cameron, it really was not a problem to take both children out to the therapy center. It got us out of the house and we always planned errands for after Cameron's therapy. I really liked the therapy center and the staff there. I especially enjoyed seeing Donna, the receptionist, who always took time to chat with me and really was one of my best support people. Over the course of the first year of Cameron's therapy we adjusted well to attending the center and when we were advised to add occupational therapy to Cameron's schedule we sought out care at the therapy center as well. Then when Cameron needed speech therapy we again chose to receive services at the therapy center.

Around the time we added speech therapy, when Cameron was eighteen months old, we were advised during one of Cam's semiannual IFSP (Individualized Family Service Plan) meetings, that is conducted by our Early Intervention coordinator and attended by all of Cameron's therapists, that Early Intervention was moving towards home based therapy. Their philosophy was based on the concept that therapy should occur in a natural environment. I can see where that can be beneficial to some children and families, however the therapy center was working for Cameron and I was hesitant to change. Cameron had grown to trust his therapy team, I was used to the schedule, and I did not want strangers coming in to our house for therapy purposes. This however was not an option when it was recommended that Cameron receive two speech sessions per week. We were told that it would not be approved unless we were willing to have one of his speech therapy sessions in our home.

I did not agree at all with the reasoning behind the push to a home based therapy program. I especially liked the fact that at the center if Cameron had a 9 am appointment then he went into therapy at 9 am and he was finished at 10 am. We were called if a therapist was sick or needed to cancel. It was run very professionally which was what I expected. I was pretty adamant about not wanting therapy at home for other reasons as well. We had had a very bad experience with a home therapist and I was resistant to try again.

I will explain the experiences we had with home based therapy and I think it will make it clear why I wanted only center based therapy. When Cameron was just over one we sought the assistance of a speech therapist/feeding specialist. The speech therapist at that time at the center did not have any openings in her schedule so Early Intervention sent a therapist to provide therapy in our home. From our first meeting I did not feel like this therapist was professional. She arrived twenty minutes late but I excused her tardiness due to coming to our home for the first time—maybe she was not sure exactly where we lived. The next visit she was forty-five minutes late, no call. This normally would not be a problem but she was specifically coming to help with Cameron's feeding issues and so we timed the appointment so Cameron would be hungry. If anyone has ever had a child with feeding issues they know how timing is half the battle. Cameron was so hungry and after twenty minutes of waiting for his therapist to show up I ended up having to give him a bottle which of course eliminated his hunger then for his session. When his therapist finally arrived she acted completely nonchalant and did not offer a reason for being late. The next week she was late again. This time my husband was off and we were all waiting around for her to come. After Cameron's appointment we were going to go to the park with the kids. Well, Cameron's appointment time came and went. Again, Cameron grew hungry and we ended up feeding him a bottle. After thirty minutes the therapist called. She was at Babies R Us and wanted to pick up a food chopper for us to use when preparing food for Cameron. My husband said okay and when he hung up I said to him that Babies R Us is over forty-five minutes away. So his therapist finally arrived for Cameron's therapy session, almost two hours late. This continued until I reached my breaking point. Our last session that we had was really something. This therapist had a three-year-old daughter and had been telling me all about her and decided on her own to bring her daughter with to Cameron's therapy session. When they arrived she said she brought her daughter to play with Abby while Cameron had therapy. When I say this turned out to be a nightmare therapy session I am not exaggerating. Her daughter proceeded to throw a tantrum because I would not let her and Abby go outside and play in our yard unsupervised. She was crying and screaming. When that was over she wanted a snack and then proceeded to take out every possible toy in our house. By the time the session was over I was exhausted and irritated. Cameron and I did not benefit at all from yet another therapy session. I called our service coordinator and explained what happened and canceled any further visits with this therapist. Of course this would not be an isolated bad experience of home therapy. Something more was to come.

After Cam began his speech therapy at the center it became apparent that he would benefit from additional speech therapy. His speech therapist had openings in her schedule and would be happy to add a second session per week for Cameron. This change however required a change to Cameron's IFSP and would require the approval of Early Intervention. I knew this would be an issue since Cameron was receiving so much of his therapy at a center. At the meeting I was informed that Cameron could receive an extra speech session weekly but that it had to be done in our home. Early Intervention would absolutely not approve another center based therapy. It really angered me. I did not feel like this was in Cam's best interest and yet I had no say in the matter. Yes we could receive a second session at the therapy center but it would require us to pay out of our pockets. Cameron's speech sessions cost $288.00 per hour and we could not afford to pay another $1,000 per month for health care costs. We were already struggling with our existing medical bills. Reluctantly, I agreed to one home based speech therapy per week. Our service coordinator, Katie, was aware of our previous experience and was very careful to select a therapist who was committed to providing consistent, professional therapy for Cam. Katie let me complain about the system to her and she did sympathize with my concerns. She, however, could not bend the rules. It was a policy of Early Intervention and she had to enforce it. I understood her positioning completely.

Cam's home speech therapist was nice and seemed genuinely committed to helping Cameron achieve his communication goals. The first few weeks she arrived on time for Cameron's therapy sessions and gave me great ideas on things to work on with Cameron. She was very kind to Abby too. Abby was developing a growing interest in sign language and so each week she would teach Abby and I some new signs to work on with Cameron. Cameron was reaching a point of extreme frustration due to his lack of communication skills so sign language became a wonderful outlet for his frustration. He could do some simple signs and we understood what he wanted. It really was working for all of us. But like all good things, after about two months, our experience changed. His home therapist missed a therapy session without calling us. I tried to reach her without luck and left a message. It was disappointing because we waited around all afternoon and she never arrived. Of course a few days later she called and profusely apologized and stated she had been so sick that she had missed all of her appointments. We accepted her apology and figured it was an isolated occurrence. A few weeks later, she called to say she would be approximately thirty minutes late for Cam's session. Tim was working from home and took the message and relayed it to me. I woke Cameron up from his nap and told him that he was going to have speech therapy. He ran downstairs and waited by the window. The therapist usually came at 3 pm but we knew she would be there at 3:30. When she did not show up at 4 pm we tried to call her but she did not answer. We left her a voice mail message and waited. Tim had just finished work and we all waited around. Finally at 5:30 pm we gave up. Tim tried her again and again, no answer. We were upset and left our house to go to the park. We never received a call from her all weekend long. By Monday I was very upset. She had missed Cam's therapy and did not have the decency to call us. It was wrong. We were in our final three months of therapy prior to Cameron turning three and transitioning to the school district. Each therapy session mattered. We were committed to helping Cameron and it was frustrating to have another therapist who did not share this same level of commitment. Finally Monday afternoon I left her a message and told her I was quite upset by her lack of consideration. If something had come up we would have appreciated her calling us to cancel rather than leaving us hanging. About one hour after I left that message she called. Imagine how bad I felt when she told me that after she called to say she was running late she got a call that her son was involved in a car accident. I felt horrible and apologized. She said it was actually very minor and he was totally fine. He did not even go to the emergency room. I did not say another word but felt like she could have called us at some point to explain this rather than waiting a few days and getting an angry message from me. Of course I did feel really bad. Two sessions later she missed again, no call. I called Katie, our service coordinator. I had had it. Katie left her a message. This time she said she was sick and had her daughter, who is sixteen-years-old, call everyone to tell them she was canceling. The funny thing is that we did not get a call. I gave her one more chance and she then ruined it. Not two weeks later she was supposed to come. It was the July 4th holiday weekend and I specifically asked her if she planned on coming the Friday (June 30th) before or not. She said yes, she was working and would be there. Abby, Cam and I turned down an afternoon play date and stayed home and waited for her to arrive. She never showed up. I left her a message and she did not call until Monday. She said she assumed we were not meeting due to the holiday weekend but would be happy to come right over. I said no to just forget it. I called Katie and I reported this therapist. Katie felt very badly. She had explained to her at the start that we were a family committed to getting Cameron all of his help, that we had had a previous bad experience with home based therapy and that she would need to commit 100% to Cameron's therapy. She said she understood but she never fulfilled that commitment. She was so unprofessional and as a result Cameron missed several critical therapy sessions that we cannot get back. The fact that she did not feel like providing Cameron with his therapy was a priority is so maddening. He deserves to be treated with respect and he deserves to receive his services. She let him down and she did not care. She never bothered to call and apologize. She honestly did not care. And I felt sad each time that she missed an appointment because Cameron had excitedly waited for her by the window only to be forgotten.

I will explain that we did have a great experience with one home therapist from the start and she deserves to receive recognition. Around one year of age Cameron was evaluated for developmental therapy purposes and he qualified to receive therapy once a month. Cameron was assigned Jamie and she was awesome. Jamie worked with Cameron for almost two years. She was enthusiastic, knowledgeable, professional yet fun, and very supportive of me. She was very committed to providing her patients with the best therapy she could and she has helped Cameron to make enormous strides in terms of his developmental goals. When Jamie started working with Cameron, Cam never played with any toys. He would only bang toys together or throw them. Well I am pleased to report that Cameron plays with toys and really enjoys playing. His favorite toys are his matchbox cars, which he now has three full cases of. Tim loved matchbox cars as a little boy as well. Cameron will sit and play twenty minutes at a time with his cars and thoroughly enjoys them. In addition to playing cars, Cameron also loves to engage in pretend play with Abby. Sometimes I will watch Abby feeding her doll or making a dinner for a group of dolls and then Cameron will join in and imitate her. He loves to also play grocery store and runs through the house pushing his grocery cart.

When Jamie first started coming, Cameron did not smile or make joyful noises while he played. He really just did not enjoy toys. Now you can hear him laughing, imitating car sounds, "talking" to the baby dolls throughout the day. It is the most wonderful sound you can imagine—hearing your child excitedly playing with toys.

Jamie was also been a great support person to me. She listened when I expressed my concerns about Cameron. She let me cry and did not make me feel bad for expressing how I felt. Jamie also provided us with ideas for how to encourage cooperative play between Abby and Cameron. Sibling rivalry peaked when Cameron was almost two and a half years of age and Jamie had great suggestions for how to minimize conflict between Abby and Cameron. We are so grateful to have had Jamie involved as a key member of Cameron's therapy team.

After we notified Katie about the troubles we were having with the home speech therapist we felt stuck in terms of what to do for Cameron's final seven weeks of Early Intervention speech services. He would age out of the system at three years of age and he would transition to our school district program for his services. We wanted him to receive his second speech therapy per week and so we reluctantly agreed to try another home based therapist. Heather was a speech therapist with a neighboring school district program and wanted to add a child to her case load for the remainder of the summer, so Katie shared our situation with her and she readily agreed to take Cameron as a patient. Well we could not have been happier with Heather and her services. Like Jamie, Heather was professional, caring, and very knowledgeable and 100% committed to helping Cameron. We really enjoyed getting to know Heather and saw great progress with Cameron during the almost two months she worked with him. She was always on time for his sessions, very engaging, and she taught me so much in terms of ideas of how to increase Cameron's communication skills. Of course I was sad that we had not met Heather sooner but I could not change the past and truly felt grateful to have Heather's help during the remainder of Cameron's service period.

All in all, we benefited greatly from both Jamie (developmental therapist) and Heather (speech therapist). However, I still feel very strongly that a family should be able to choose what they feel is best for their own child and situation in terms of where therapy is received. Early Intervention is an amazing resource for families and each and every therapist who agrees to be an EI provider needs to make a 100% commitment to helping children become the best that they can be. They need to hold themselves to the professional standards that are set forth by EI and to be able to work independently without constant supervision. Each therapist also needs to understand that the manner in which they conduct themselves can positively or negatively impact the reputation of Early Intervention. When all is said and done, I am very grateful for the help Cameron and our family received from Early Intervention. Without Early Intervention Cameron would not be where he is today. The only thing that I do wish is that the two home therapists that we had bad experiences with would have realized the importance of their positions and how much Cameron was depending on them to provide him with the quality of services that he is entitled to and deserves. And I also wish that I would have spoken up sooner and not allowed the situation to continue for as long as I did. I could have rectified the situation sooner if I would have expressed my concerns immediately to Katie rather than keep giving the therapists multiple chances.

Loving Cam is Easy ... Everything Else is Hard!

Over the past four years I have had people ask me if it is hard to have a child with special needs. That is such a tough question to answer because it has a no and a but component to it. Let me explain. My no answer is because it is not at all hard to love Cameron. I love both of my children equally but differently. I remember when I was pregnant with Cameron wondering if I would be able to love him as much as I loved our daughter. I remember reading the poem about loving two children and actually putting that in Cameron's scrapbook. And I can tell you that throughout the pregnancy I fell in love with Cameron just as I had fallen in love with Abby. I loved feeling him kick and dreaming about what he would like, what his personality would be and how Abby and him would play together. I remember the first moment I laid eyes on him—I was smitten. He was everything I had dreamed he would be. And he was ours. I remember feeling so in love with him and so in love with Abby. I actually felt like my heart had doubled in size. And I will never forget the night he was placed on the ventilator and baptized prior to his transport to a Chicago-area hospital. I felt my heart breaking. The thought of losing Cam was unbearable. I had only known him for one week in my arms and thirty-seven weeks in my stomach and yet I could not imagine my life without him. And even now when I think back to those scary moments I feel myself start to well up with tears. I love Cameron so very much. I can honestly say that my love for both of my children is equally strong but there are different things about each that contribute to that love. Although they are brother and sister they are unique individuals and I cherish each of their uniqueness. I can also honestly say that the only thing I wish I could change about Cameron is the pain he had to experience as a newborn. I often wonder if he remembers all of his spinal taps, the ventilator, the various IV, etc. I wonder if he remembers being in a hospital isolette rather than in his crib in our home. My hope is that he does not. My fear is that in some way he does. Regardless, other than that there is nothing I would change about my amazing Cameron.

My but answer has nothing to do with Cameron but everything to do with his special needs. What I am referring to is the financial pressures of his medical care, the coordination of all of his therapies in relation to our HMO insurance with Early Intervention, and the realization that some people will never see Cameron for who he is rather than the disability he has.

One of the hardest parts of having a child with special needs is the financial pressures associated with his medical care. In addition to his pediatrician, Cameron sees a pediatric neurologist, a pediatric pulmonologist, a pediatric ENT (ear, nose and throat), a pediatric orthopedic specialist, an ophthalmologist and an allergist. He also used to see a physical therapist, an occupational therapist, speech therapist and developmental therapist until he turned three and entered the school system. As an HMO patient, any visit that Cam has besides the pediatrician requires a referral. And there are limits to which specialists he can see, which hospitals he can receive tests at and how many therapies he can receive per year. The HMO plan that we have is very expensive, it is the most expensive insurance plan that my husband's employer offers. It also provides the best coverage of services, hence the cost. Our HMO plan allows Cameron to receive sixty combined therapies per year. That sounds like a lot of sessions but when a child receives multiple types of therapies per week these visits are exhausted very quickly. Additionally, the therapy referrals are given as bundles. Sometimes Cam's speech therapist would use her visits and send in a progress report and request for more visits to find she was only approved for two more visits. That means that not only did we miss some visits while we were waiting for the referral to be approved, at times we waited three weeks, but his therapist also had to write another progress report and submit it for more sessions. It was actually a very frustrating process because it interfered with continuity of therapy when we were having a few weeks of break in therapy as we waited for another approval. And forget about calling the hospital referral person directly. I made that mistake and she let me know it. I ended the call by telling her that if she was a mother of a child with special needs who desperately needed therapy she would understand my frustration at all of the red tape. Again she told me not to contact her directly again. Nice, isn't it? And we pay an enormous amount of money to be treated with such disrespect. If I sound angry about this it is because I am. In all of my years working never could I treat a customer with such disrespect and maintain a job and yet I have found when you are dealing with medical insurance it is a totally acceptable standard of service. And that is sad, it really is.

Early Intervention procedures also posed some challenges for us due to our HMO coverage of therapy visits. In the state of Illinois all children under the age of three who have been assessed to be at risk for developmental delays are eligible to receive services through Early Intervention. A family is charged a monthly service fee based on family income to help cover the cost of the services. We are thankful to have had Early Intervention due to the limitations of our insurance. We did, however, face some challenges. Because we had insurance that did cover some therapy it felt like we were penalized in a sense. When Cameron was waiting for approval for a referral he could not continue with therapy because EI would not cover his visits until a referral was formally rejected by our HMO. And our HMO would not cover the visit until they had formally authorized it. If our insurance did not cover any therapy sessions then Cam would not have had the constant interruption in services during the referral waiting period. He would have received all of his therapy and it would have just been covered through EI. So it was actually detrimental to us to have had some coverage from our HMO.

And the last part of my but response is that it is so hard to have a child with special needs and have them seen for who they are. Cameron is an amazing four-year-old toddler who captures each and every person's heart with his smile. He is active, mischievous, loving, and funny and above all he is strong willed and determined. He is determined to live life to the fullest and not let anything slow him down. And yes, he just so happens to have cerebral palsy. I will never forget the day that I had a physician refer to him as the patient with cerebral palsy. She did not even bother to stop and see what his name was because she thought nothing was wrong with identifying him as his disability. That angered me and continues to anger me when people label him. And now I do correct people. When this physician did that I corrected her but did not educate her to understand why the way she was speaking to Cameron was wrong and unacceptable. Just because Cam has cerebral palsy it does not define who he is. It is a part of his life but it is not at all who he is. Some days I can eloquently educate people and some days I can impatiently correct them. Unfortunately, I am a mom and some days my heart is too sad to be so eloquent. Regardless of how I get the message out, when someone labels Cameron they do walk away knowing that he is not cerebral palsy. He is an amazing little boy who just so happens to have cerebral palsy. Recently I thought of a great phrase to help express this concept and it is "Please do not label me, rather enable me to be everything that I can be!"

Unrealistically Expecting Others to Make Me Feel Proud

I have spent a lot of time feeling sad about the lack of support I have often felt from people these past four years. I expected certain people to call and check on Cameron, to ask if they could help us with Abby, and to celebrate when Cameron took his first steps. Most recently when I found the strength in myself to sit down and share Cameron's story with the world by writing this book, contacting the newspapers and giving presentations, I expected so many people to find my work exciting and to be interested in hearing all about it. I was devastated when a beautiful article ran in the Northwest Herald about Cameron's journey and my book that I was writing and people who read the article and knew us well could not stop to say they even read it. I was also sad when I shared a very touching nine minute video montage of Cameron's journey with so many friends and family and again, only a few people took the time to say they even watched it. Since I am a person who always stops and acknowledges others accomplishments and I go out of my way to call and say great job or I am thinking of you during a hard or sad time, my expectations were that each and every person who knew us and our family would do the same. To take one minute and reply to my e-mail with a link to the video montage and say it was touching, amazing, moving, or anything else would have helped me so much. Unfortunately, only a handful of people did. And although I do appreciate all of the people who did take time to tell me how proud they were of me and all of the work we had to done to help Cameron, I have wasted a lot of energy on feeling angry at the people who did not bother to contact me. My expectations were that every single person I e-mailed would contact me.

I now know my expectations were very unrealistic, not only regarding the most recent newspaper article and video montage incident, but many other situations over the past four years. However, I finally know why my expectations were as high as they were. These past four years of my life have honestly been the hardest and most trying times that I have ever experienced. There were days where I felt a sense of helplessness that is indescribable. Many mornings I had to drag myself out of bed to face another day of uncertainty after having spent hours crying myself to sleep. I felt so many feelings that I could not explain to someone who has never had the experiences that we have had with Cameron. I can honestly say that my emotions ranged from guilt, anger, despair, helplessness and loneliness to extreme pride, gratitude, elation, and triumph. Some days were really good days, days when Cameron was making so much progress and I could feel the happiness and thankfulness that we had Cameron in our lives and he was doing as well as he was. And some days were really dark days, where no matter how much I told myself how lucky I was to have Cameron and to see what he was accomplishing, I still was not able to feel joy or purpose. I was able to meet the needs of my children, both of my children. I was able to take care of them, laugh with them, and fulfill all of Cameron's therapies and medical appointments in addition to juggling a part time job and home responsibilities. I was, however, not able to enjoy my life, to laugh a true laugh, to smile a true smile. My heart hurt and my body hurt. I was in more pain than I had ever experienced in my life and despite trying, nothing seemed to help with those feelings except time.

Today I can say I feel much stronger emotionally. I do have many good days, where not only does my mouth smile but so does my heart. I laugh from my belly and feel a carefree feeling as I play with my children outside. The good days are far outweighing the bad days. But, the bad days still are bad. And they still hit me without warning. Sometimes the bad days are for only two to three days and sometimes they linger longer. I still get up every day, I still take care of my children, and yet I cannot see the blessings of that day or of my life, no matter how hard I try to tell myself how truly blessed I am. Someday I hope to say that every day is a good day, maybe scattered with some bad moments, rather than bad days. For now, I will take each good day and be thankful for it and weather each bad day with the unbeatable strength and spirit that has helped me come this far. I have found talking about my feelings really does help on those bad days and I have learned that I need to focus on today and not worry about all of "the what ifs" that tomorrow might bring and all the "wish I would haves" of yesterday.

So, I do have to say that because of the extremely sad times I have had, I had high expectations that each and every person that knew us would praise my work and make it a point to tell me what a great job I was doing because I needed them to do that. I used to be a person who felt great pride in myself and did not have to look externally for that type of recognition. For now I need external praise, I need people to tell me I am doing a great job and that I am making a difference in the lives of others by sharing our story. I do not know why I cannot feel my pride on my own. But hopefully with time I will learn that it really does not matter if others tell me I have done a great job, that my book is wonderful to read, that Cameron's video montage that I spent many hours and poured my heart and soul into making is touching and beautiful, because I will feel pride in myself without the need for others to feel it. And so, after four long years of feeling disappointed in what I perceived to be the lack of support of others, I have finally realized that the disappointment that I am feeling is actually due to my own lack of ability to feel proud of all that I have done to help Cameron be everything that he can be. It truly does not matter if others are proud of me or not. The only thing that matters is that I know in my heart that I have done everything that I can to help Cameron and to create a life for our family that is filled with unconditional love and happiness.

I cannot write about how hurt I have sometimes felt due to my unrealistic expectations without mentioning how truly awesome many people have been to our family. We have had the support of many family members and some very good friends these past four years. We have had countless phone calls and e-mails to ask us how Cameron is doing, to check on us and to ask about Abby. We have had special surprises arrive in the mail for Abby (thank you Stephanie and Eric) and that has meant the world to her and to us. Most days I am able to focus on the fact that we are truly blessed to have so many supportive people in our lives. It is so comforting to know that at anytime we have a number of people we can call and gather strength from. I have watched as some of our family and friends have cried alongside of us during those sad times and celebrated just as enthusiastically as we have during those miraculous moments. I have watched as our cousins and their children have grown to love both Abby and Cameron and truly enjoy the time they spend with them. At a recent family birthday party my cousin Christopher spent a good part of the party playing with Cameron. He took Cam to the park and played and played. He sat by Cam and listened to Cam's cd when Cam wanted to listen to the music and they shared a bag of skittles. I watched in awe. Chris is a twenty-one year-old college student and he gets it. He feels the joy in knowing and loving Cameron. When I told a good friend about this I cried. I cannot even begin to explain how emotional it makes me when I see someone embrace one of my children and truly care about them.

Abby and Cam love spending time with their cousins ... here they are with Pat, Katie, Chris and Nicholas

Another example of amazing support came from my goddaughter and cousin Ali. Ali is fifteen-years-old and absolutely loves Abby and Cameron. One day I decided to write a letter to some area newspaper reporters to share Cameron's story with them. I wanted to share our story so that we could make others aware of how important it is to have hope when you receive a devastating medical diagnosis for yourself or a family member. I was quickly contacted by Regan Foster, a reporter with the Northwest Herald and she expressed interest in meeting Cameron and our family to write an article about him. It was so exciting and we shared the news with all of our family and friends. Regan then notified us that Cameron's story was going to be on the cover page of the local and region section of the paper and we let everyone know. When my Aunt Sandy (who had been by my side at the hospital when Cameron was placed on the ventilator) told my goddaughter Ali that Cameron was going to be in the paper and which section Ali told her "Mom, Cameron deserves to be on the first page of the entire newspaper, not on the cover of an inside section. He has worked too hard to not be on the cover." My Aunt Sandy called me to tell me what Ali said. I love my goddaughter! She completely recognizes how hard Cameron has worked to get to where he is and wants to see him receive recognition for his accomplishments.

Cam always smiles when he is around Ali!

I am also so thankful that my brother, Scott, and my sixteen-year-old niece, Rachel, stop by often to visit and to help relieve some of the stress. It is always a welcome relief because Scott and Rachel just laugh and laugh at Abby and Cam which always lightens my mood. Scott loves how active and daring Cameron is and sometimes he just sits and shakes his head as Cam climbs onto the kitchen table, the window sills or the back of the couch. He cannot believe how Cam is so steady and never falls. Of course Cam loves making his Uncle Scott laugh so he shows off even more. Sometimes if Scott stops over to visit on his way home from work and Rachel is not with him Cam will get so upset and keep asking Scott where Rachel is. I will always remember one day when Scott stopped over and the kids were playing in the yard with my mom. He snuck up on them and took the hose and got them so wet—they were laughing and screaming. After that, anytime Scott would stop over and they were in the yard they would beg him to hose them down. Abby always says that she loves seeing Uncle Scott because he is so silly. When Uncle Scott and Rachel leave Cam will beg them to stay and keeps asking them to play more. And Abby and Cam love the times that Rachel comes to stay overnight—they love to wake her up early in the morning. Rachel plays the entire time with them and never seems to get tired.

Hanging out with Rachel   Relaxing with Uncle Scott!

And so each day I can choose to waste a lot of energy on being angry and disappointed with the people who are not as involved in Cameron or our family's life as I had hoped they would be or I can cherish all of the wonderful memories I am building of all of the people who love Cameron with all of their heart. And to each of you I say thank you! You truly might not know how much your gift of love and caring for Cameron and our family means to us, but let me assure you it has made this journey possible!

A Gallery of Special Pictures!
A Day at the Beach

When I decided to write this book I knew from the start what my title would be and envisioned in my mind the cover. I contacted Shannon Curcio, a local photographer, and asked her if she would be interested in taking the photos for our family and she readily agreed. We had met Shannon a year earlier when she was expanding her photography to include children with special needs and she provided our family with a free session at our home and pictures of Cameron. She was so friendly and so good with Abby and Cameron and we learned that she had been trained as a special education teacher as well as a photographer. Shannon met our family at the Crystal Lake Beach just ten minutes from our house one Saturday morning and here are some of the amazing photos she took. She also deserves credit for the cover photo as well, which she took this same morning. Shannon graciously donated her time to provide our family with these amazing photos that you see below. We are forever grateful for her generosity and her amazing ability to capture such beautiful pictures that we will forever cherish. Shannon is a freelance photographer and all of her beautiful work as well as contact information can be found on www.curciophoto. com.

Our Heartfelt Journey!

Deciding to Share Our Story with the Medical Community

Ever since Cameron got sick at one week old I had told Tim that I wanted to know what the purpose of Cam being sick was. Why did this happen and what were we meant to do because of it. I remember thinking about families who lose a child and yet go on to create foundations to help others. How do they do that? How do they suffer such a loss and yet find the strength to go on and make someone else's life better? I asked Tim why some people find meaning in a tragedy while others never regain their will to continue on with their life. I also remember telling Tim that maybe someday, when I felt stronger, I would make a difference.

It is funny but up until recently I have always felt like I have not known what I was meant to do with my life. Yes, I am a mom to Abby and Cameron and they bring me an unbelievable amount of joy and happiness. But yet I have always felt like there is something missing in my life. I can finally say that through our journey with Cameron I have found my purpose. I want to educate the medical community about how important the manner in which they deliver a medical diagnosis to a patient or a patient's family is because of the impact it can have on that patient's future. We had two extremely different experiences with neurologists for Cameron and we learned firsthand how much of a difference this could truly make. I also want to give other families with children with special needs hope. I honestly believe that because we had hope we were able to arrange the therapies and provide Cameron with the support that has made him who he is. I am not at all implying that if every family with a child with severe brain damage does what we did their child will have the same abilities. However, I do believe that if every family with a child with special needs has hope and gets Early Intervention services for their child that they will maximize their child's potential and they will enable their child to be the best that

that child can be. I recently read a quote by Christopher Reeve that summarizes my belief so well—"By choosing hope, everything is possible!" There is so much truth to this statement as was evident by how Christopher Reeve chose to live his life after his accident. He chose hope and he accomplished so much as a result. We chose hope too!

On June 24, 2006, after Abby and Cameron went to bed, I sat down to write a letter to Dr. Shah, Cameron's neurologist. Here is the letter I wrote:

Dr. Shah,

I am writing to you to ask for your opinion on a project I would like to work on and present at area teaching hospitals and medical schools. As you know the experience we have had over the past two and a half years with Cameron has changed our lives dramatically. The journey that we began when Cameron was born has taken us to a place we never expected to go—and yet we honestly cannot imagine our lives any different than they are. We feel so blessed to have Cameron in our lives and feel like having a child with special needs has made us so much more aware of what is truly important in life. Cameron's struggles have made us stop and re-think so many things that we took for granted. We have learned to appreciate the little things and understand that no matter how much we would like to we truly cannot control what happens in our lives or our children's lives. We do however strongly believe we have the ability to make a difference in their lives—as we have seen with Cameron these past few years.

The main reason why I wanted to get your opinion on what I would like to do is because we honestly feel that Cameron has done so extraordinarily well due to your overall philosophy. From the moment we met you in 2003 and you were reviewing Cameron's MRI with us and honestly telling us of the extensive brain damage you saw—you were able to convey a message of hope to us rather than doom and gloom. I will never forget asking you will Cameron walk, will he talk, will he have any quality of life…. and rather than guessing or worst yet telling us no—you gave us an answer that has driven all of our efforts these past two and a half years—you told us "The day you say Cameron will never do something, he never will!" You did not give us false hope but you gave us hope to know that you and no one else could predict his outcome and future abilities. I also remember you strongly recommending that we begin therapy immediately—and that with therapy we could maximize Cameron's healthy areas of his brain to help compensate for his damaged areas. You said to us—when Cameron reaches a year if we find that he is developing right on track then nothing will have been lost by getting intervention early. However, if we take a wait and see approach then we might miss an important window of opportunity to really help Cameron learn how to compensate for his deficits. You spent over two hours with us—letting us ask you the same questions over and over, allowing us to cry and grieve and never once making us feel like we were imposing on your time. From that first meeting we knew you would be an important part of our family's life. You gave us hope when many other physicians would not have. There were many times during that first year while we awaited Cameron's diagnosis that we felt helpless and hopeless. At times when Cameron did not make progress in therapy it was hard to stay focused and believe that what we were doing would be beneficial. Each time we felt like giving up we remembered what you told us—and we looked at Cameron and knew he deserved every opportunity to become the best that he could be—whatever that would be. You educated us about Early Intervention Services and made us aware of what types of help were available for Cameron. We honestly had never heard of Early Intervention prior to meeting you.

The project I would like to work on is a presentation for me to deliver to area teaching hospitals and medical schools. The overall message of my presentation will be about delivering bad test results to parents in an open, honest manner while giving those parents hope. When you told us of Cameron's brain damage you never once minimized the severity of it—but yet you gave us hope to think that he could do things that others might say he could not. You told us to always believe he could do something unless he shows us otherwise. It is sad to think that if we would have had a different neurologist delivering the test results what a different outcome we might have had with Cameron. The reason we know this is due to the fact that when Cameron initially got sick at day six of age—with suspected meningitis—and was transported to a Chicago-area hospital on a ventilator—the initial evaluation by one of the neurologist there was not positive. He told Tim and I that Cameron had no functionality and we should never have had him put on life support. We were devastated and actually left Cameron's bedside to go home and prepare our families for this outcome. It was not until an attending physician called us to come back and spent hours with us observing Cameron that we regained our hope. As it turned out after finishing fourteen days of antibiotics Cam was discharged and we were told he was perfect—no long term effects would come of his meningitis. As we now know that was not the case—the brain damage showed up later during Cam's readmission to Lutheran General. We are so thankful that Cameron was re-admitted to Lutheran General and you were assigned as his neurologist—because had we had the other neurologist we know the prognosis we would have been given would have been grim and we would not have gotten all of the therapy that we did for Cameron. So for our family—we have learned truly firsthand how much a physician's diagnosis and prognosis can truly influence how a family cares for a child, and ultimately that child's future. Because we had hope from you—we made sure to get the Early Intervention services that truly made a huge difference in Cameron's life. We do understand that regardless of how much intervention a family gets that sometimes the outcome will not be as positive as Cameron's—but the key is that every child deserves to be given every opportunity to be the best that they can be and that Early Intervention is designed to provide such opportunities to children.

My hope is that from you I can obtain some of the MRI images that show the extensive damage that Cameron suffered as well as the explanation of the areas that are being viewed in those images. I am then going to create a proposal to send out to area teaching hospitals as well as medical schools along with these images and a video that we are going to have made of Cameron. For us this is a step towards healing the sadness that surrounded Cameron's first year of life. Sadly I cried every single day of Cameron's first year—the unknowns of his future, the unknowns of how he got sick and always wondering if we missed something along the way. I feel like if I can make a difference in how physicians deliver messages to parents—that I can make a difference in the lives of many children. And although I wish that Cameron would have never had to have gone through all that he has—I will know that what he has endured has made a difference for others. My goal is not to gain anything financial from these presentations, strictly to gain personal satisfaction knowing that I might make a difference in the lives of other children and their families.

I would really like to speak to you about my idea and see if you think that it is something that is feasible. As far as credentials, in addition to having a B.S. degree in Psychology with a minor in Biology, I hold a Masters degree in Public Health with an emphasis in Health Promotion and Education. I have four years of professional training experience, teaching classes to adults that averaged twelve students and lasted from two to five days in length. And most importantly, I am Cameron's mom and have dedicated myself to making sure that he is given every opportunity to become all that he can be!

Thank you for taking the time to read this Dr. Shah!

Sincerely,
Becki Enck

After I wrote this letter I saved it and went to bed. On Tuesday, June 27th I decided that I wanted to fax the letter to Dr. Shah. I knew that if I did not send it right away then I might never gather my confidence up again to send it. Tim faxed the letter for me. Imagine my surprise when I received a call from Dr. Shah later that day. I was excited and amazed. Dr. Shah is the director of Pediatric Neurology at Advocate Lutheran General Hospital. He has a very full patient load and yet he not only had read my letter but took time to call me. I remember him saying how much he appreciated the letter and that he agreed with my idea and wanted to help me deliver my message to the medical community. I also remember him saying that we gave him way too much credit. Of course I had to tell him, no, we do not give you nearly enough credit. He is a very humble man and never looks for recognition for the amazing work he does. And yet he so deserves to be recognized! We talked about some ideas and we decided we would talk further at Cameron's August 11th appointment. When we hung up I was excited. I immediately called Tim to tell him the great news. He was so happy to hear that Dr. Shah had called and liked my idea as well.

I decided to create a video montage of Cameron's journey. I wanted to show through pictures Cameron's progress from birth. The saying that a picture is worth a thousand words could not hold more true. When you see some of the pictures displaying Cameron's abilities you are reminded of this. I worked on the montage for a few weeks. I needed to select pictures that would show Cameron's progression and would highlight all that he is. I wanted to include pictures from therapy as well as with Abby. I also wanted to make sure that each picture that I chose was worth a thousand words. Luckily I had many, many pictures to choose from. Because I enjoy scrap booking, I had taken so many pictures the past three years. The problem became how I select just a few pictures from literally thousands of pictures. I took my time … looking at each picture and thinking about what it represented … what story it told. I had only made one montage before. A few weeks earlier I had happened upon a Web site and decided to create a montage for Tim for his birthday. I created a three minute montage with pictures of Tim with Abby and Cameron and ordered a DVD of it for Tim's birthday. He loved it. It was a very sentimental gift and turned out well for a first time attempt. This time I had more time to work on the montage and had bigger plans for it. I told Tim that my goal was to share Cameron's journey with the world so I wanted this montage to be phenomenal. My plan was to order many copies of the DVD and send them out to newspapers, magazines and even Oprah. I knew that if I created a slideshow that documented Cameron's journey while inspiring hope in the people that viewed it then it would capture the heart of someone to make it public.

Selecting the music for Cameron's montage proved challenging. I searched many nights on-line for just the right songs. I listened to various cds that we owned. Although I have many favorite songs, not one of them would work for our message. Then one day I found the song I was looking for by accident. The Crystal Lake Public Library was hosting a children's concert with songwriter/artist Kathleen Gibson. My mom and I decided to take Abby and Cameron to the concert. Both of my children absolutely love music and I thought they would enjoy the concert. Imagine my surprise when Cameron was not at all interested in staying. I think he actually felt overwhelmed by the number of people and the sound in the room. Abby did not want to leave and so my mom said she would walk around with Cameron while we listened to the music. Kathleen was an animated presenter. All of the children and adults were laughing and participating in each song. As her final song Kathleen sang "One Love is All we Need." She had all of the children stand up by her as she sang. As I sat and listened to the song I remember thinking—this is it—this song would be the perfect song for the first half of Cameron's montage. It was such a moving song. I actually had to stop myself from crying.

After the concert ended Kathleen stayed to sell copies of her cds and Abby and I chose three cds to purchase. Abby really enjoyed the concert. I waited until everyone else had paid and as I was paying I decided to share the project I was working on with Kathleen and see if I could use her song in Cam's montage. Kathleen was very interested in our story and readily agreed to allow me to use her song. She also was interested in meeting Cameron and so my mom brought Cam in. Cameron was much more comfortable now because most people had left and it was quiet. Abby told Kathleen how much she liked her guitar playing and Kathleen asked Abby and Cam if they would like to play her guitar. They were excited and so she took them over to her guitar and allowed them to play it. They loved it and ever since then Abby has been asking me to buy her a guitar. I told her we should definitely put that on her Christmas list and if Santa brings her one someday we could ask Kathleen to autograph it for her.

After we got home from the concert and Abby and Cameron went down for their naps I worked on the montage. I uploaded Kathleen's song into the montage and pressed play. I was absolutely in awe of what would follow. Words cannot describe how perfectly Kathleen's song fit with Cameron's journey pictures. It was the right fit for sure. I spent a few more hours working on the video and then sent Kathleen an e-mail with a link to it. Here is a copy of the e-mail she sent back to me after viewing Cameron's montage. It meant so much to me that I printed and saved a copy and am sharing her words here with you:

Dear Becki and family,

I am humbled and honored that I am in some small way a part of your gift to the world, to all those who will be touched by your offering of love and wisdom.
Please keep me posted! You and your children are an inspiration to me, and to many, many others, I am certain!

In hope and harmony,
Kathleen Gibson
www.kathleengibson.com

After speaking to Dr. Shah I also decided to write about what happened to Cameron so that I could create a proposal for my presentation idea. The first night I sat down and wrote ten pages about Cameron and realized I had so much more to write about. It was then that I jokingly said to Tim that I could write a book about our journey with Cameron. I was joking at the time but Tim said why not. He was serious. He always complimented me on my writing skills throughout our marriage and now he was telling me to go for it, to just write a book. I reminded him how hard it was to write a ten to fifteen page paper in college and that I could never write a book. He reminded me that in college I was writing about a topic someone else chose and someone would be grading. If I wrote a book it would be about something I held near and dear to my heart and no one would be grading it. That was true. I went to bed that night thinking about what we talked about. He was right. This would be very different than writing a term paper. And I would have no deadline. I could write whatever I wanted whenever I wanted to. It would be a great story to give to Cameron some day whether I ever pursued having it published or not. And it would possibly help me deal with some of the feelings that I have had these past few years. The past few years were very hard at times, there were so many unknowns. And yet they were what made me who I am today. I was tested to my limit. There were many days I did not know if I would be able to do what I needed to do and yet I had no choice. I had to persevere. I loved Cam with all of my heart and I needed to give him everything that I could. And so I decided to write this book. I even decided to tell our family and friends about my idea. I believed in my heart that if I put my mind to it not only would I write this book but I would have it published. Some people might have thought I was naïve, and I was, but nonetheless I was determined to become an author.

One of my good friends, Amy, was very supportive when I told her of my idea. She had been worried about me the past few months. I just did not seem the same. I was very stressed out with our move and really worried about Cameron's upcoming transition to preschool. I thought I was hiding it well but not to her. She remarked about how excited I seemed about writing my book as well as possibly delivering presentations to medical professionals. And as I talked about my ideas she saw a glimpse of happiness return. I had really felt lost the past few months. I was feeling sad, anxious, and stressed out and tired. I just did not feel motivated to do much because nothing was helping me feel fulfilled. Abby and Cameron were keeping me busy but yet I truly felt like something was missing in my life. I did not really have a passion for something that would define me as a person separate from my family. And all of a sudden I found that passion. I wanted to share our journey with others. I wanted every-one to see Cameron and what an amazing boy he was. I wanted to tell everyone about Abby and how she was the best big sister to Cam. And I was ready. I was at the point in our journey where people would see the progress Cameron had made. I knew every detail of what had happened. My mind was clear and I was focused. And as you can see, I fulfilled my goal. This book is proof of my efforts to find my purpose.

Another friend who encouraged me was Leigh Anne. Leigh Anne and I met at a park district program the summer prior to Cameron starting preschool and quickly became friends. Her boys, Devan and Dustin, and Abby and Cameron are the same ages and each time we get together the kids have a great time play-ing and Leigh Anne and I have a great time talking. Leigh Anne is a very good support person to me when Cam has struggled with impulse control issues. She is able to give me suggestions that are practical for Cameron. Leigh Anne has allowed me to be completely open and honest with her about my fears and concerns without being afraid of being judged. During the past year when I put my book down and stopped working on it because various medical issues arose with Cam she would gently remind me of it and the importance of getting it published. Needless to say when I finally decided to self publish this book and told her the great news she was ecstatic. And she was honored when I asked her to write a letter to Cam to be included in this book. Little does she know that the honor is truly ours that she was willing to write a special letter that our family will forever cherish.

I decided to notify area newspapers about Cameron's journey in hopes that they would want to share his story and help to make parents of children with special needs and the medical community aware of how important it is to have hope. I sent a few e-mails and was pleasantly surprised to get an immediate response from Regan Foster, a reporter with the Northwest Herald. Regan read my e-mail immediately upon receipt and then viewed Cameron's video montage online. She e-mailed me to let me know that she was very interested in meeting our family and Cameron and wondered if we would have some time in the next week to meet with her. We were so excited and set up an appointment with her for the end of the week. She would arrive in the morning to talk to us and meet Cameron and then in the afternoon a photographer would come to take pictures.

The night before Regan came I was excited and nervous. I knew that the article she would write would have an impact on so many people and I was excited. The project I began early in the summer was moving very quickly and was really gaining momentum. Regan was going to be able to help us reach a lot of people very quickly and that was exciting.

Abby and Cameron were very excited for Regan to arrive at our house. It was so cute because every time I would go to check by the front door they would follow me to the door. Regan arrived right on time and Abby and Cameron were jumping up and down as she walked up our driveway. They love when people come to our house and they greeted her with huge smiles. We decided to sit in the basement to talk because the basement is finished and is the playroom. Regan was so friendly and easy to talk to. She asked questions about when Cameron was born, when he first was sick with suspected meningitis and what happened after that. As we talked she laughed as she watched Abby and Cameron running all around and playing. Cameron loves to slide down the play slide and so he was busy showing her how he could slide by himself. He then decided that he wanted to impress her more and he created an obstacle course where he moved his slide over to the play house window, then moved their play table over by the slide. He proceeded to climb onto his table, up the steps of the slide, slide down the slide and dive through the window into the play house. Regan loved watching him in action. She marveled at his abilities and his friendliness. As Cam realized that he was making Regan laugh he showed off more. He "sang" Jeopardy and Happy Birthday for her. He played peek a boo through his playhouse window and giggled with his sister. He was in such a playful mood and Regan really enjoyed his spirit. Abby also talked quite a bit to Regan and even showed her some of the signs she had learned recently. Of course we made sure we told Regan what an amazing big sister Abby is and how she was even learning sign language to help Cameron communicate. When Regan left she said how much she enjoyed meeting our family and hoped we liked the article that she would write. She was not sure when the article would run, but she promised to call us the day before.

Abby and Cameron wanted to play outside before lunch, but we changed their clothes since the photographer was not coming until the afternoon. After playing on the swing set I gave them lunch and down for a nap they went. When Cameron woke up he was still in a very playful mood and was so silly while I tried to change his diaper and his outfit. Abby was also laughing and acting silly. We went downstairs to have a snack before the photographer, Scott, was to arrive. When we got downstairs, the doorbell rang and Scott was here. His timing really was perfect. He took a lot of pictures of Abby and Cameron playing first in the basement and then outside on the swing set. We were not sure what picture he would use for the article but we were anxious to see.

A few days passed and Regan called to ask one more question—Tim and my ages, and then to tell us the article would be running the next day, on Thursday. I called some of our local gas stations and found out that the Northwest Herald would arrive at 3:30 a.m. Tim and I went to bed so excited to read the story the next day. Although I fell asleep I woke up at 2 a.m. and then could not fall back asleep. I waited until 3:00 a.m. and then woke Tim up to tell him I was going to go to the local gas station and pick up some copies of the paper. He laughed but thought it was a great idea and said he would wait up until I returned. I went to two gas stations, the second of which had the paper and quickly paid for a few copies and went out to my car. I could not wait until I got home to read the article so I quickly found the local and region section and there we were. Regan wrote a wonderful article about Cameron and our journey. She began the article with "A blonde ball of energy in khaki overalls" and I laughed so hard. How true, how true! She captured Cameron's spirit in her first sentence. She went on to share Cameron's story and our message of how important it is to always have hope. I read the story twice and then headed home to show Tim the article. He loved it and was so excited. Scott chose to include a picture of Cameron trying to go out into the back yard while I was still trying to get Abby's shoes on. We ended up buying twenty-five copies of the paper because we wanted to save five copies for ourselves and then we needed to send copies to each of Cam's doctors as well as many family members and friends. It was so exciting to know that Cameron's story was now public and we had the potential to positively impact many people. After the story ran Abby and Cameron made special thank you pictures to send to Regan and we also sent her a picture of Cameron.

Our First IEP

Prior to Cameron starting our school district's at risk preschool program we met with the school psychologist and social worker to talk about Cameron and our family. We were able to ask a lot of questions about the program, the teachers and therapists and what we could expect in terms of Cameron's daily schedule. Tim and I felt many different emotions about Cameron transitioning to the school district. We were excited because we wholeheartedly felt like Cameron was ready for this new beginning. He was ready to move from individual therapy to group based therapy. He was ready to be around other toddlers his own age. And he was ready for some independence from Mommy, DaDa and Abby. Of course we were also very nervous about Cameron's transition. We were going to be stopping all of the therapies that were working for Cameron and start a new program. Cameron was comfortable with his routine, he loved each of his therapists and we all knew what was expected of us. Transitioning to the school district would mean an entire new team for Cameron and new expectations for him as well as us as a family. And we were particularly worried about Cameron's severe food allergies. Our home is completely peanut and tree nut free and we know Cameron so well that we can tell if his asthma is starting to act up or if he is not feeling well. All of a sudden other adults were going to be in charge of making sure Cameron was safe in terms of the foods he had access to as well as his breathing status. I knew in my heart the staff at his new school would take his health concerns extremely seriously but I was still apprehensive to let him out of my sight. Change can be scary no matter what, but especially when you have a child with serious medical issues and limited communication skills.

Our IEP (Individualized Education Program) meeting was scheduled for Friday, September 15th. Cameron would be turning three the following Monday, September 18th, and be ready to start school. The week of his IEP meeting was also the ending of each of his therapies. We contemplated what to do to thank each of his therapists for all of their hard work and we decided to write each of them heartfelt thank you notes and include a special picture of Cameron. We hoped that these notes would be something that they would cherish and hold forever. On a difficult day the note would serve as a reminder to the impact they were having on the children and families they were working with. Cameron said good-bye to Robin, his occupational therapist that he had worked with since he was one-years-old and Dana his speech therapist that he had worked with since he was eighteen months old on Monday. On Wednesday, Cameron had his final developmental therapy visit at our house and we said good-bye to Jamie. Jamie brought Cameron a birthday gift and a special gift for Abby. Abby felt so very special that Jamie had remembered her as well Cam. Jamie allowed Abby to be an active participant in his therapy sessions and really worked hard to make Abby feel important during Cameron's therapy sessions. As Jamie left our house I sat down and cried. I felt so sad to be saying good-bye and yet I knew we would continue to keep in touch. On Thursday, Cameron had his last home speech therapy with Heather. Although we had only worked with Heather for seven weeks we really had grown attached to her quickly. Like Jamie, Heather was able to include Abby in Cameron's therapy sessions and always listened as Abby talked to her. Heather surprised Abby and Cameron with gifts as well. And as Heather left I started to cry so hard. She actually forgot to take her notebooks with her and I had to call her on her cell phone to come back to get them, but Tim ended up taking them out to her car. I was too emotional to see her again. Again I knew we would be keeping in touch with Heather but nonetheless ending therapy with her was difficult.

The night before Cameron's IEP meeting I could not sleep. I tossed and turned. I wondered what services the school district representatives were going to recommend for Cameron and what criteria they would use to qualify him for placement in the program. There are twelve different criteria that can be used. I learned about the criteria from Angela, our parent liaison with Early Intervention. Angela was going to attend the IEP as a support person to Tim and me. I had known Angela since Cameron entered the EI program and Angela and I had spent many hours talking over the past two years about having a child with special needs, the challenges of therapy, and the transition process. Angela's son Dylan was already in our school district program, so she was a great source of information and support to me during the months leading up to Cameron's IEP meeting. She also suggested we write a letter to read at the IEP so that the staff would get to know Cameron prior to starting school. I loved her idea and I did write a letter to read at the meeting.

The morning of the IEP meeting I took Abby and Cameron to our local Burger King to play in the play area while Tim worked a half of day from home. We stayed out until Tim finished work and then we came home for lunch. Tim gave both kids baths and put new clothes on them prior to putting them down for their naps and I gathered everything that we needed to bring to the meeting, including Cameron's medicines, medical permission forms, our letter to the staff and pictures of Cameron that we wanted to share. At 1:15 pm my mom arrived to watch the kids and Tim and I left for the meeting. Although our meeting was scheduled for 2 pm we arrived at the school at 1:30 pm. We were both a bit anxious and wanted to make sure we arrived in plenty of time. Around 1:45 pm Angela arrived and we chatted until the meeting started at 2:00 pm. When we were told it was time for the meeting I felt a surge of anxiety. I took a deep breath and Tim and I held hands as we walked into the meeting room. A few staff members were already there and so we sat down. In addition to Tim, Angela and I, seven other school representatives attended the meeting. We met the special education administrator, the occupational therapist evaluator, an occupational therapist, the school social worker, the school psychologist, Cameron's teacher, and the school nurse. Everyone was very friendly and after they introduced themselves I felt completely at ease. Each attendee read their report on Cameron and made recommendations as to what services Cameron would benefit from. Tim and I were asked after each presentation if we wanted to add anything else. After everyone made their presentation and recommendations, we were asked if we wanted to share anything else about Cameron with them. I decided to read the following letter that I had written:

Staff of Glacier Ridge,

We have been preparing for this day for almost eleven months now and it is hard to believe that it is already here. Last October I attended the transition informational meeting hosted by our Early Intervention office and when I came home and we sat down to talk about Cameron transitioning into the school district we made a very large and important decision for our entire family. Based on many conversations with Cameron's therapists, Angela, and many parents of children attending the Crystal Lake School district at risk preschool program, we moved three miles so that Cameron could enter this program and for both of our children to receive an education through District 47. It was a very big decision and yet we knew it was the best decision we could make for our children and their future. (At this point a few staff members laughed and said oh my, we have high expectations to live up to!).

This past week has been filled with so many emotions. We have said good-bye to Cameron's therapy team that has been with us since Cameron began therapy at four months of age. It was a bittersweet week—the fact that Cameron has excelled in each of his therapies and is so ready to now participate in the district preschool makes us so excited for him and all that this upcoming year will bring. However, we also feel sadness in leaving the team that has helped make him who he is today. We are leaving our comfort zone as much as Cameron's. Up until now every decision we have made in terms of Cameron's therapies has proven to be the right ones—Cameron has really thrived with the interventions he has been given. We are now changing our entire routine and although we know we are doing the right thing for Cameron, it is a bit scary as well. In our hearts we know this next year is going to be filled with unbelievable moments for Cameron and we look forward to watching him grow and change. We look forward to working with each and every one of you. We are excited for you to get to know Cameron, his big sister Abby and both of us. As a family we are committed to helping each other be the best that we can be! We want you to know that any and all suggestions that you have, any piece of advice you can give, will always be received with an open mind. We truly respect that each and every member of Cameron's new team will continue to help Cameron to thrive and to be everything that he can be.

We want to share a few things about Cameron so that you can begin to get to know him before you meet him next week. The first thing is that Cameron is a sweet little boy who will smile and laugh his way into your hearts. He is very affectionate and not only loves to receive hugs but openly gives them in return. He thrives on praise and will proudly shout "I did it" after he has accomplished something.

Cameron is quite the funny little boy too. When he laughs, he laughs from his belly and some days you will find him filled with giggles. His laugh is often quite contagious, as you will soon learn.

Cameron is really enjoying exploring the world and trying to figure things out. He is quite inquisitive and very often fearless. He does have excellent climbing skills but sometimes he lacks any form of fear to realize that he is putting himself into a dangerous situation. He also is very interested in seeing how everything feels, tastes, and smells. Therefore a lot of times you will still see him mouth the toys he is playing with and we have to be careful because he will even put small pieces into his mouth. You will also see Cameron smell things often—especially food. Although he continues to be open to trying new foods, he is cautious. He always smells something first and often it takes several attempts for him to build up his courage to taste something. He does have severe food allergies, peanut and egg, so we will always send snack with him to school and we will never send something that we have not tried at home. If you do notice him become itchy or red and blotchy—he might need a dose of Benadryl due to minor allergies as well. Cameron is doing a great job with self feeding, but often times he is too busy to sit long enough for a meal. So he will eat a little and run and eat a little and run. He loves to use a fork and spoon now too. He will let you know if he has gotten something on his hands that is making him feel uncomfortable for you to wipe it off for him. He is also doing great drinking from a cup with a straw and very interested in drinking water from an open cup. Sometimes he finds it more fun though to spill his water on the floor and watch it run all over. Again, praise really does help and seeing other children doing something will be a great motivator for Cam as well.

Cameron does get overly excited sometimes and is not quite sure what to do with his excitement. It is at these moments that you might see him throw a toy or go to hit. It is not at all motivated by anger, but just an uncertainty of how to express his excitement. We are working at home to teach him to clap, shout hooray or even jump up and down, but in the midst of an exciting moment that is not what always comes to mind. Cameron will say sorry after he throws a toy because he will quickly realize it was not an appropriate thing to do. He really wants to please each and every person and then will feel bad if he upsets someone.

Cameron has an enormous amount of energy and will typically go from activity to activity very quickly. He can sit and play with one toy for a longer period of time when we are sitting interacting with him—but if left to his own will just run and run. He typically will nap and sleep very well at night—but there is little down time during the day.

In the morning I can sometimes tell when Cameron is having a disorganized day. I will make sure to communicate that to you in the notebook. We are finding that using his oral vibe and his Nuk brush can sometimes help, as can chewing bubble gum. There are days where he will reorganize himself but then for whatever reason there are days he will not. We are open to any suggestions for calming that you might have and will share different ideas we come up with that we find helpful as well.

Lastly, Cameron is a very determined little boy. Despite many medical obstacles he has done so very well and worked so hard to achieve each and every one of his milestones. We have watched in awe as he survived suspected meningitis at one week of age, endured twelve spinal taps, survived a severe asthma attack and ICU hospitalization at fourteen months of age and many other medical procedures and crises along the way. He has a determination and spirit that is unstoppable and admirable. His biggest obstacle right now is communication and although it is hard for him he is intent on speaking and signing to help you understand him. Sometimes he will try to point or whine for something, but he knows he has to attempt to say something before he is given it. Of course each attempt brings lots of praise. We typically will tell Cam he needs to use his words or let him show us something and then have him say it as well when we are uncertain of what he is saying.

We are so proud of Cameron and are excited to share our amazing toddler with you. We hope that each day that you work with Cameron you walk away with a smile knowing how much of a difference you are making not only in his life but in our family's lives as well. We respect each and every one of you for committing to help the children of our community to become all that they can be. Thank you!

After I read my letter everyone complimented Tim and I on what we had done so far in terms of all of the help we had given to Cameron and they all took time to look at the special pictures we chose to share with them.

Now it was time to hear the qualifying criteria for Cameron. I held my breath. I was not sure what would be selected as the reason and felt some anxiety about it. The program administrator explained how a child needs to meet certain criteria to be included in the program and read through the criteria and the team each acknowledged that Cameron did meet the qualifications. His criteria was defined as global developmental delay. That was not a surprise to either of us. Tim and I have been aware of Cameron's developmental delays since his first set of Early Intervention evaluations at three months of age. We knew he was significantly delayed in many areas and we agreed to accept their criteria for inclusion in the program.

After qualifying Cameron into the program, we listened to the recommendations of what services Cameron would receive. He would be a participant in the four day preschool program, which would meet from 9:00 am—11:30 am

Monday through Thursdays. He would also receive an extra sixty minutes of individual speech therapy weekly and twenty minutes of individual occupational therapy per week. This was in addition to group therapy time that he would be receiving while class was in session. We were asked if we agreed with the recommendations and we did. We felt very confident in each team member and what they were recommending for Cameron. We were also assured that if Cameron showed signs of needing additional services that his IEP could be modified at anytime. We then signed all of the paperwork for Cameron to enroll in our districts at risk preschool program.

The final portion of the meeting involved us meeting Cameron's new teacher, Miss Jeanie, and setting up a visit appointment. We decided to set up Cameron's classroom visit for Tuesday, September 19th since both Tim and I would be able to attend with Cameron. That would mean that Cameron would start school the day following his visit. Miss Jeanie gave us a cute postcard to give Cameron from her and also his supply list. As we left the meeting we felt great. We felt confident that our decision to move to this district was the right one and that Cameron was ready for this next experience. We hugged Angela and we promised to keep in touch. We were lucky in that we would be able to see Angela around school since we would no longer be in the Early Intervention Program. Once a child turns three they age out of EI. And I also was lucky because Angela and I developed a friendship that extended beyond EI and so I was confident that our relationship was not ending but rather just moving in a new direction.

When we arrived home Abby and Cameron were excited to see us. They came running to the door and both yelled surprise. We handed Cameron his postcard from his new teacher and he looked at it and smiled. Then Abby took his postcard and ran and got some tape and she hung it on our refrigerator so Cameron could see it. Abby asked all about Cameron's teacher and the school. We told Abby Cam's teachers name and she started to have Cam practice saying it so he would be ready for his first day. All in all, the entire transition process from EI to the school district went very smoothly. I will be honest though in saying that it was an extremely stressful process just from the stand point of so much change. We also had sold our home and purchased another home during this process, which really added stress. But in the end, I can say with 100% conviction that we made the right decision to move into the Crystal Lake school district and we really could not have asked for a better transition period or IEP meeting. It all had fallen into place very nicely. Now all that was left was dropping Cameron off at school and leaving him. I was of course nervous for his 1st day of school to come, but also excited about it.

Happy 3rd Birthday Cameron!

For some reason as Cameron's 3rd birthday approached I found myself feeling so emotional. I am sure if it was because my baby was growing up and getting ready to start school and soon would not need me as much as he had. He was ready to have some time apart from us so that he could make his own friends and learn how to behave with other children. I knew in my heart Cameron was ready for all that was to come and yet I was sad because I knew that he was getting older and would need me less and less. His first two years were filled with so many doctor appointments and therapy visits that I felt like I never had a break. This past year his doctor appointments had lessened and he had started to play a little on his own. He was growing slightly more independent, and although I cherished his emerging independence a part of me felt a sadness knowing that my baby was growing up. I sat down a few times to write Cameron his birthday letter and found myself crying as I thought about the past year. Finally, on his actual birthday, I was able to write him his special letter.

Cameron,

As I sit down to write you your 3rd birthday letter my mind is filled with so many amazing moments from this past year. It is hard to describe how I am feeling at this moment. I cannot believe that I no longer have a little baby to take care of. You have grown up so much this past year and have gained so much independence. It has been so much fun to watch you explore your world and figure things out for yourself. I hope that when you read this letter someday you will realize that you have accomplished so many amazing things this past year.

One of your biggest accomplishments this past year has been your communication skills. At the start of this year you could say a few words such as Hi, DaDa and Bye. Now at three you can say so many words

114

such as BeBe (for Abby), Mommy, Mama, Milk, Up, Down, Potty, On, All Done, Thank You and I Did It, to name just a few. At the start of this year you were still very frustrated at your lack of communication. You would hit your head on the floor or throw things if you could not tell us what you wanted. Now not only can you say many words but you are also doing a great job with signing what you want. You have been learning sign language at speech therapy and Mommy, DaDa and Abby are also learning to sign with you as well. At first we were worried that if we signed to you, you would not have a reason to talk. We quickly learned the opposite to be the truth. Signing and speaking to you together have helped to motivate you to talk to us because you love that we can understand you. A moment I will forever cherish and never forget happened on May 9th. I was getting ready in the bathroom and you walked in and said "HI Mama!" I started to cry. I could hardly believe what I was hearing. For the very first time you called me MaMa. You always called me DaDa and would laugh. And when I would say, no I am not DaDa I am MaMa you would laugh and call me DaDa even more. I will never forget hearing your beautiful voice call me MaMa. You now call me Mommy as well. I love when you run up to me to tell me something and say Mommy.... it is such a beautiful sound!

Another big accomplishment for you is that you have learned to really play with your toys and enjoy them. Your favorite toys are your Matchbox cars. You have over 100 cars now and everyday you play with your cars and your garage. You also have started to imitate Abby. If Abby is playing in the pretend kitchen you follow her and do everything that she does. You will pretend to eat play food, drink from a cup and feed Abby's baby dolls. It is so fun to watch you and Abby playing together.

This past year we have learned that your passion is music. You received a cd player for your 2nd birthday and quickly took a liking to it. You know how to turn the player on and off, adjust the volume and the song and you even will carry the CD player around with you. You love all types of music and you know which cd is which just by looking at it. You also love to dance to music and you are a great dancer. We have found that you can hum songs that you have only heard once—so imagine our surprise at 2 am one morning when DaDa and I were awakened to you humming the jeopardy tune. You watched Jeopardy the day before and woke up and were singing. All of a sudden I woke up to you singing and then realized what you were singing. You even make your voice go up and down at the right part of the song. Everyone loves to hear you sing Jeopardy and the attention you get from it inspires you to sing more. You have also learned how to sing Happy Birthday, 10 Little Monkeys Jumping on a Bed and Sticky, Sticky Bubble Gum. Someday we are certain you will be a musician!

Of course your physical skills continue to amaze us. You have learned to climb on top of the kitchen table, to climb onto our window sills and on to the back of the couch, as well as anything else you see. If you want something, you will now move a chair over to what you want to help you climb higher. You are also able to navigate our entire swing set with ease. Even the rock climbing wall that you initially struggled with you soon mastered after just a few weeks. You love to run and I have to admit at this point you can outrun Mommy, DaDa and Abby. You think it is a fun game, especially when we try to change your diaper or put your pajamas on for bed. You take off running all through the house and now you know how to run so we cannot get you. You used to run right into us—not anymore. Sometimes you will tease us and run right up to us and then take off—so we almost catch you but then can't. It is so funny to hear you laugh so hard as you escape. Needless to say when we go out a lot of times we do have to put you in the stroller just for safety reasons if we will be in a parking lot or a crowded area.

Now that you are three-years-old, you are going to be starting pre-school. I look forward to seeing you make your own friends and cannot wait to hear all about your day and see all of the beautiful artwork you create. And of course I cannot wait to sing many new songs with you. Mommy is so excited for you and of course a bit emotional about this next step for you. But I do know you are ready and it will be a fun experience for you.

Happy 3rd Birthday Cam!

Love Always,

Mommy

Since one of Cameron's favorite toys are cars we decided to have a cars theme birthday party. We would invite our family to our house for dinner and dessert. Originally we planned his party for the Saturday prior to his birthday but ended up canceling the party a few days before. Tim and I were feeling very overwhelmed with Cameron's therapies all ending and his impending IEP meeting that we decided to call our family and re-schedule his party for two weeks after his birthday. I wanted to enjoy his party and with his IEP meeting the afternoon before I knew I would not be able to enjoy preparing for his party. All of our family understood. It was the first time we ever canceled a big event, and yet we knew it was the right decision because we really wanted Cam's 3rd birthday to be a wonderful celebration and to enjoy every moment of it.

In addition to a family birthday party we decided to have a kid's party as well. Cameron had become friends with Abby's friends from school as well as their siblings and so I decided it would be fun for him to have his own little birthday party. Since McDonald's continues to be Cameron's favorite food to eat, I decided to have his party at the McDonald's near our house that also had an indoor climbing area. We invited ten children total, including Abby and Cameron, as well as the moms. I decided to have the party from 10 am—Noon on a Friday because none of our friends had preschool on Friday. I also knew that Cameron would be tired from his first few days of preschool so I wanted to have an early party so that he could go home and take his nap afterwards. I was very excited to be having Cameron's first kid's party. When I mailed out his party invitations I mailed one to Abby as well. I never realized how excited she would be to receive an invitation in the mail. When the invitation arrived Abby started jumping up and down and thanking Cameron for inviting her to his party. It was so sweet. She then hung her invitation on the refrigerator for everyone to see.

Cameron's party had to be scheduled through the McDonald's corporation. The woman who schedules the parties was so helpful. Due to all of Cam's food allergies I needed to check if the birthday cake they provide had nuts as an ingredient or even traces of nuts. She double checked the ingredient label for me. She then told me to go in to the restaurant to pay the deposit and the remainder of the party costs would be due on the actual party day.

Two weeks before the party I went into McDonald's early one Saturday morning. I was so happy to see one of the managers that Abby, Cam and I had become friendly with over the past three years. Christina was always so nice to Abby and Cameron and always made sure to stop and talk to us whenever she saw us. During Cam's first three years we were frequent visitors to McDonalds. Because this McDonald's was near to the therapy center where Cam attended therapy, we often would go through the drive through for my morning diet coke and Abby loved the apple dippers. Sometimes we would stop after Cam's therapy and we would go into the restaurant and sit. Christina always took time to talk to us and got to know us. She knew how sick Cameron had been and always remarked how well he looked. She would ask Abby what was new and all about her friends. Abby really loved seeing Christina and if we stopped in and Christina was not there Abby was sad that she had missed seeing "the nice lady" as she often called her. Of course when I stopped in to pay the deposit for Cam's party Christina immediately came up to me and asked where the kids were and how they were doing. She genuinely cared about them and wanted to hear all about them.

After Christina and I talked for a little bit I asked her if she had read the recent article in the newspaper about Cameron and our family. Unfortunately she did not see it so I promised to bring it in to her the next time we came. As we chatted another manager came up to us, Chuck. I also had seen Chuck on many occasions and he was always friendly to us. Chuck overheard me ask Christina about the newspaper article and said "I read it—I was amazed at that little boy!" I of course had to share with him that the little boy he read about was my son and he was even more interested. He said the story really touched his heart because he had a three-year-old grandson. He showed me a picture of his grandson and talked about how awesome being a grandfather was. Then I told Chuck that we were really excited because Cameron was about to turn three and we were going to have his birthday party there. Then Chuck took the check that I had given Christina and handed it back to me. He told me that the restaurant would like to host Cameron's 3rd birthday party for him. I was so touched and speechless. As I took the check back from Chuck I became all choked up. What a caring and generous gesture he made. He was so happy to hear that Cameron would be celebrating his special birthday at their restaurant. I was so touched. I thanked both Chuck and Christina and left. As I walked out to my car I started to cry. I could not believe how incredibly thoughtful Chuck and Christina were. Of course it brought back memories of the generosity that McDonald's Corporation had shown us when Cameron was only a week old and on life support. During Cameron's hospitalization for suspected meningitis I lived at a Ronald McDonald House so that I was minutes rather than almost one and a half hours away from Cameron. I had often heard about the Ronald McDonald Houses and thought they were such a great idea, and then when I lived there I realized how truly awesome and what a blessing they were to families with children who are ill. So not once, but twice already in Cameron's lifetime, McDonald's has so generously helped our family. We are touched beyond belief and so thankful for the corporation's generosity.

Cameron's party at McDonald's was so much fun. He had ten other children attend, including his big sister Abby. He loved playing in their big play area—climbing through the tunnels, sliding down the slide and running after his friends. All of the children enjoyed their happy meals and the Ronald McDonald cake. Christina was working the morning of Cam's party so she helped set everything up and serve lunch and cake. She was so excited when we arrived and I was able to take a picture of Abby and Cam with her. All of the moms that attended helped me so much with the party and when it ended we all agreed we had a great time. That evening I ordered pictures from Cam's party and put together special thank you mini albums for Chuck and Christina as well as a letter to the McDonald's Corporation. I wanted to make sure to thank all of our friends at the Crystal Lake McDonald's as well as the corporation as a whole. McDonald's gives back so much to our communities and it is vital that as a recipient of its' generosity we were able to send a proper thank you.

Here is Cam at his McDonald's birthday party with Abby and our friend/assistant manager Christina.

Cam's First Day of School

Cameron was so excited about his first day of school. Whenever I would say to him that he was going to be starting school he would sign on, he associated school with music. He had helped to drop Abby off at school the year before and there was a cd player in her classroom. Cameron assumed that he would also have a cd player in his classroom and that he would be listening to music during his school day. Imagine how happy Cam was when we took him for his classroom visit and to meet his teacher, Miss Jeanie, and there was a cd player in his classroom too. He could not contain his excitement. Music is definitely Cameron's passion and if we allowed it, he would listen and play with his cd player all day long every day. Although music is a wonderful enjoyment of Cam's, we do have to limit his listening time because he will only focus on the cd player and ignore all other opportunities for play. So although we were excited to see a cd player in Cameron's classroom as well, we were a bit nervous about it too. Cam loves to control the player—at home he changes cd's, the volume, the track. He is in control. We knew that in his classroom that would not be allowed. The teacher would have to be in control and we wondered if Cameron would be able to accept that. During our visit it became apparent that Cameron could not leave the cd player alone and so Miss Jeanie did have to put it away so that Cam could explore the classroom and meet his classmates. Since the cd player is used during circle time we knew that Miss Jeanie would have to creatively think of a way to teach Cameron that she was the only one allowed to touch it. Tim and I wondered how Miss Jeanie would do this, but we were confident that she would find a way to teach Cameron what he was allowed to do and what he was not allowed to do in his classroom.

Cameron's visit went so well and Tim and I enjoyed meeting Miss Jeanie, the aides in the classroom as well as the five other children that would be Cameron's classmates. We felt confident that Cameron was really going to enjoy going to school but we expected there to be some tears. Over the summer Cameron had started to show signs of separation anxiety. If I was going out in an evening after Tim got home from work Cam would stand by the door and cry. He would go back to the door every few minutes and say "Mommy" and look for me. I wondered how Cam would react to me leaving and was a bit worried. I knew that if he started to cry when I handed him to his aide that I would break down and cry too. I had experienced this a year earlier when Abby started preschool and when she cried walking into her classroom so did I. I just felt so emotional and anticipated the same feelings with Cameron.

Cam with DaDa before our first visit to school

Cameron started school on Wednesday, September 19th, the day after we took him for his classroom visit. My mom came in the morning to take Abby to preschool so that I could take Cameron and not have to rush then to get Abby over to her school. Cam seemed excited. He had his backpack on and he was ready to go. He said good-bye to Abby and Me-Mom as they left and then I put his shoes on and we got into the car. As we drove to school I told him we are going to school and you are going to have so much fun. He started to say music on and sign it and I told him yes, you are going to listen to music at school. You are also going to go play with your friends, paint, eat snack and listen to stories. When I told Cam they were going to eat snack he signed eat and said eat. When I told him he was going to play he also signed play. He was really listening to me and seemed excited. When we arrived at school we parked and walked over to the doors. Since Cameron is attending our school district's at risk preschool program, many of the children arrive on the school bus and parents are not allowed to walk their children to the classrooms. If you drive your child then you are met outside by a classroom aide and they will walk the child to their room. Cameron and I arrived a few minutes early. We put his backpack on and we walked hand in hand across the parking lot and up to the entrance door. Cam let go of my hand and went up to the door and looked in. He then started to knock very loudly on the door. He wanted to be let in. He was ready. He kept pounding and I started laughing. It was quite funny to watch him. All of a sudden one of the classroom aides came to the door and she was laughing too. She said she was happy to see that Cam was so excited for school. I introduced myself and Cameron. She took Cam's hand and he turned to me and said "Bye Bye Mommy" and off he walked into school. I could not believe it. No tears, just huge smiles. He looked so excited. He was ready and he felt comfortable. As I walked across the parking lot to my car I could not help but start to laugh. Cam's reaction was completely opposite from what I had expected. I thought that he would cry. I thought he would be nervous. Never did I imagine that he would feel that level of confidence to walk right in to school with a classroom aide he had never met. It was such a feeling of relief.

After I got in my car I immediately called Tim on his cell phone. I knew he was waiting at work to hear how Cam did. When I told him that Cam was standing at the door pounding to get in he laughed so hard. He could not believe it. He too had imagined that Cam would cry because he had been more attached to me lately. He said he felt relieved. As I hung up it hit me—both of our children were now preschoolers. It seemed strange. I now had two children in school and once a week I would have a morning to myself. Abby attends preschool Monday through Wednesday and Cameron attends preschool Monday through Thursday. I work on Mondays and Tuesdays so that means on Wednesdays I have two and a half hours to myself. It was the first time in four years that I would have a morning free to myself. Tim told me that he wanted me to enjoy my free time, he did not want me to do any school errands and he did not want me to go home and do housework. He said go and enjoy your time. Go to a bookstore, a coffee shop, take a walk, but whatever you do enjoy your time because you have earned it. That made me happy because he recognized how much I needed a little time to myself to relax. Tim recognized how hard I had worked these past four years and how all consuming being a mom can be. And he wanted me to take time to re-charge and re-energize. I decided I was going to take time for me and not feel guilty about it. Thursdays I would have time with just Abby. I decided that Abby and I would make this our special mommy and me time. I was not going to take Abby out to run errands. Instead, each Thursday Abby could decide what she wanted to do with her mommy. She could pick a park to go play at, a bagel shop to go and relax and eat bagels together or games she wanted to play together at home. I could not wait for our time together. I knew it would be special and something we would both cherish.

After I dropped Cameron at school I went to a local farm market to meet my mom for breakfast. She was excited to hear how great Cameron did with going into school and we had a chance to sit and chat. It was a relaxing morning and I enjoyed spending time with my mom. I told her how I could not believe that both of my children were now in school—that although at times time did seem to drag as they were little now they were growing up and it was only a matter of time before they would both be in school full-time. It was a bittersweet feeling to think of how big they were getting.

After breakfast, I ran over to a local coffee shop to read the newspaper and then headed back to Cameron's school to pick him up. I got there early and sat out on a bench right by the playground. It was a beautiful, sunny day out and I really enjoyed sitting peacefully. All of a sudden I saw Cameron and his class come outside to play in the playground. Although I was sitting right there Cam did not see me. His aide and his teacher did and both gave me a thumbs up. He proceeded to walk over to the slide and climb up and slide down. Then I watched as he sat in the fire truck and rang the bell. He still did not see me and his teacher walked over and sat on the bench by me. She told me Cameron had a wonderful first day, he listened very well and he did not cry at all. She said he even played with another one of the boys in class and participated in the entire circle time. She said he could not have had a better first day. I told her thank you—thank you for coming over to talk to me and for obviously making Cameron feel so comfortable and so welcome in her classroom. After five more minutes of play it was time for the children to go home. Many of the kids ride the bus and the aides started taking them to their buses. Cameron's one on one aide, Miss Carolyn, walked him over to me and when Cameron saw me he yelled out Mommy and then he said "I DID IT!" He was beaming with pride and had the biggest smile I have ever seen. Miss Carolyn told me that he had a wonderful day and that they enjoyed him so much. Cameron gave me a big hug and together we walked hand in hand to the car. He was so happy and I asked him some questions about his day.

When we arrived home, Cam looked a bit tired so I gave him his sippy of milk for the car ride home and when we got home he said Wiggles. Cam wanted to watch the Wiggles while we waited for Abby to come home from school. I made both of their lunches and Cam and I sat on the couch to wait for Abby. When Abby arrived she was excited to see Cameron and asked him all about his day. He told her "I DID IT!" and she told him she was so proud of him.

After lunch Cameron looked exhausted. It was nap time and although he usually takes a two hour nap he slept for three full hours. And even when he woke up he seemed tired. The rest of the day he was slow during his play, he was not nearly as active as usual. He really was tired from his first day of school. And what an amazing first day he had!

"No Abby! Mine!"

Cameron made great strides in his communication skills after he started preschool. He was signing more and more, combining signs and attempting to speak to us. We were so excited to hear new words and laughed when after the first full week of preschool he had learned two new words, no and mine. Of course some people would say oh, those are words that as a parent you never want to hear but we were so excited to hear Cam say no and to say mine. He was communicating with us and understanding that these were powerful words. As Cam began to say more words, his speech therapist, Miss Kim, also worked on his pronunciation. When Cam would say a word with multiple syllables often times you would understand the first portion of the word but the additional syllables were mumbled. He began to pronounce his second and third syllables and our understanding of what he was saying increased dramatically. Abby really wanted Cam to learn how to say her name because he called her BeBe and she kept saying I really wish Cam could say my name. I wrote Miss Kim a note in Cam's backpack asking her if she could work with Cam on Abby's name and within a week he was saying Abby. The way he pronounced it was "A Bee" but nonetheless Abby was thrilled to hear her brother saying her name.

In November, about two months after school started, Abby and Cam were playing in the basement together. I was in the office and could hear them talking to one another. One of Abby's favorite things to do with Cam was to dress up as princesses. Cameron loved the attention Abby paid to her so he would readily dress up so that he could play with his sister. Imagine my surprise, and Abby's surprise, when she asked Cam if he would like to play dress up and he said "No A Bee." She asked him again and again Cam replied "No A Bee" and he ran off to play with something else. Abby started to cry and I could not console her. When she finally stopped crying I asked her what was wrong and she told me that she was upset because Cameron was not doing what she wanted him to. I had to explain to her that now that Cameron was a preschooler and getting older that sometimes he would want to do different things than she wanted to do and she had to accept if he said no to her. She started to cry again and told me that she did not want him to tell her no. Although it was such a big milestone for Cameron to be able to communicate his wants and needs, it was also a big milestone for their sibling relationship. From this point forward both Abby and Cameron would be making decisions about their relationship, it would no longer be one-sided.

After a week of hearing Cameron tell her no when he did not want to do something, Tim and I noticed an interesting coping technique that Abby developed. She had many tears that first week of Cam's assertion of his independence, but then one Saturday morning Tim and I overheard a conversation she had with Cam. She wanted to play something and Cam did not want to and so he had told her no. She quickly rephrased her question so that the only possible answer Cam could give her was yes. We noticed that this became quite common. Whenever Abby wanted to influence Cam's decisions, she always thought out how to ask him her question so that he had no choice but to say yes. We were shocked at how clever she was and watched as Cameron struggled to figure out other ways to tell his sister that he was not interested in doing something. We started to see him run away from her and hide rather than speak to her when she asked one of her rehearsed questions. He also ignored her when he did not want to respond yes. Over time, they have both adjusted to Cam's independence. Abby has turned six and is interested in things that Cameron is not, such as playing school. Meanwhile, Cam is very into his jungle animals and can spend a great deal of time playing with them. They do still play together, but we are noticing they also willingly choose to play alone throughout the day as well. When they do play together they both participate in choosing what to play. Sometimes Cam will ask Abby to play air hockey (he calls it air tockey) and often times she will ask Cam to play grocery store with her. One thing that Cameron is really enjoying is having Abby sit and read books with him. Abby is learning to read in Kindergarten and Cameron just smiles and smiles when she sits down with him and reads him a book.

Cameron's Journey: A Story of Hope and Inspiration by Becki Enck

Dr. Shah chose to share the letter that I had sent him over the summer with Dr. Mangurten, the Director of Pediatrics at Advocate Lutheran General Hospital. One fall day Dr. Mangurten called to tell me that he had read the letter that I had sent to Dr. Shah and had presented it to the education committee. The committee decided that they would like to invite me to present Cameron's story at one of their monthly practice management meetings that the residents and medical students attend. Dr. Mangurten wanted to have an opportunity to meet with me and to discuss Cam's story in more detail. We arranged to meet following an appointment that Cameron had with Dr. Shah so that I would not have to drive out to the hospital an additional time. When I met Dr. Mangurten I immediately felt comfortable sharing Cameron's story and my reasoning behind my decision to now share our story. I learned that he was responsible for establishing the NICU many years earlier at Advocate Lutheran General Hospital and then we talked about how Abby had been born prematurely and had spent eleven days in their NICU. He was also thrilled to hear that I myself had been born at Advocate Lutheran General Hospital and had a long time relationship with the hospital because my father received all of his treatments there for a rare pancreatic disorder that he had. After we talked, Dr. Mangurten said that he would check the schedule and then contact me with a date for my presentation. As I left his office I felt on top of the world. I felt like the old Becki, confident and driven by a purpose. I felt like I had the ability to do anything I set my mind to and it was a great feeling. It had been such a long time since I had felt such pride in myself and confidence in my abilities.

A few weeks passed and then Dr. Mangurten called. He said he had really enjoyed meeting me and that I had a positive energy about me that was contagious. He wondered if I was still interested in delivering my presentation and of course I said yes! He said that the only problem that he could foresee was that the meetings were at 7:30 a.m. at the hospital and he was not sure if that would work in my schedule. I assured him that I would be able to attend an early morning meeting and that I was truly honored to have this opportunity. The director of residents, Dr. Lundblad, would be calling me with all of the details and to answer any additional questions that I might have. As I hung up the phone I knew that the door was now opening to a world of many new opportunities. These opportunities would provide me with the chance to make a difference in so many people's lives. I definitely felt and continue to feel that I have found my purpose in my life.

Dr. Lundblad and I discussed the details of the presentation. I would have forty-five minutes to present followed by a fifteen minute question/answer session. She was more than willing to make copies of my presentation materials and would make sure the conference room was equipped so that I could show Cameron's nine minute DVD video montage. She also indicated that the number of medical students and residents that attend varies based on their schedules and rotations but that a typical meeting will consist of twenty-five to thirty-five attendees. Dr. Lundblad also gave me her phone number in case anything happened that morning. I was really looking forward to meeting her and she invited me to meet her in the morning for breakfast prior to the meeting.

Tim and I decided that since we lived ninety minutes away from Advocate Lutheran General and due to the unpredictability of the weather in Chicago during December that I would drive out the day before and stay over in a hotel near the hospital. He wanted me to have a chance to relax and feel rested the morning of my presentation. It was the perfect idea. I really enjoyed having the entire day to shop and visit places that I used to go to when I grew up in the Park Ridge area. I felt so calm and relaxed. My mom and Tim kept asking me if I was nervous about my presentation and I said no. I was not at all nervous. I was excited beyond words. Although I had not formally presented for a few years, I had no concerns about it. I was excited to know that the message I was about to deliver would be heard by many residents and medical students who someday would be delivering devastating medical diagnoses to their patients and patients' families. I would have the ability to make them aware of how the manner in which they delivered the news would impact a patient's future. I knew that my words would be powerful and my message would be one they would carry with them throughout their careers. And I knew that each and every time they spoke to a patient or patient's family that they would remember Cameron and remember the importance of never giving up hope. I wanted each of them to walk away understanding the impact that Dr. Shah's advice have had on our family, "The day you say Cameron will never do something, he never will!"

I woke up on December 6th, the morning of my presentation at 4:30 am. I did not need the alarm clock, the hotel operator or Tim to help me wake up. I literally jumped out of bed and started to get ready. I felt fully rested and alert. I still was not at all nervous. I was excited. After I got ready I called Tim to tell him that I was going to check out of the hotel and drive to the hospital. He was surprised to hear that I was all ready to go. I was really early. I arrived at the hospital around 6 am and the plan was that I would meet Dr. Mangurten and Dr. Lundblad at 7 am. I sat in the lobby thinking about my presentation. I made sure that I had two copies of the video montage with me as well as a giveaway I had ordered. I wanted to give each attendee something that they could take away with them as a reminder of Cameron. A few weeks earlier when looking on the Internet I had found a gentleman who made candy lollipops with a photographic image throughout. I had contacted him and he offered to make the lollipops at cost for me and to rush order them. I just had to e-mail him the image I wanted embedded on the candy. I chose a picture of Cam in the water at the beach where he was clapping his hands. It was a picture of Cameron that I loved because at the moment he was clapping he had said to us "I Did It!" I decided to have the words I Did It! appear under Cam's image. The lollipops arrived in perfect condition one week before my presentation. Of course Abby and Cameron had to test taste them. They looked amazing. They were a cherry flavor and fully edible. I immediately called Mike from www.popartcandy.com to thank him for his help. I had a basket full of these lollipops with me to pass out. And I also made sure that I had my HOPE stone with me. About a year earlier I had found a small silver stone at a store that had the word HOPE on it. It was something that I carried with me on those very hard days as a visual reminder to always keep hope alive in my heart and my mind.

Cam loved eating a sucker with his picture on it!

At 7:00 am I met Dr. Lundblad and Dr. Mangurten for breakfast. It was so nice to sit and talk to them prior to presenting. Both of them thanked me for being willing to share Cam's story and both agreed that the message that I would be delivering was important. Dr. Mangurten said that there is so much emphasis during medical school and residency on book knowledge but unless people are willing to share their experiences about bedside manner it is something that can be hard to teach. I agreed. It still makes me so sad to think about the lack of care and compassion the first neurologist had when he delivered his exam results of Cameron to us. I honestly feel that if I am willing to share our negative communication experience then I might be able to prevent other families being spoken to in the same manner.

As we walked to the conference room we ran into Dr. Shah. He was smiling and immediately shook my hand and thanked me for coming. He was excited to hear how well Cameron was doing in preschool and to hear that Cameron could now say his name, although he pronounced it Dr. Shy. He also laughed when I told him how he tells me he wants to see Dr. Shah when I say we are going to the doctor, even if it is for an ear ache or other ailment.

The conference room was set up for my presentation and the medical students and residents began to arrive. Soon the entire room was full and there were even a few people who ended up having to stand. My estimate is that there were approximately forty attendees. I was so touched when I realized that Margie, Cameron's pulmonology nurse, came to support me and hear my presentation too.

When I got up to speak I was not at all nervous because I was going to speak about something that was so near and dear to my heart. I spoke about the importance of the manner in which a medical diagnosis is delivered to a patient and his/her family is and the impact that the delivery method can have. I emphasized how important it is to introduce oneself, to make eye contact and to not act hurried by looking at one's watch or inching toward the door. Next, I talked about what helped us the most when Dr. Shah delivered the news of Cam's MRI that showed his brain damage. I shared how Dr. Shah sat down and talked to us, he allowed us to ask the same questions over and over and he would re-explain his answers in a way we could understand, he offered his support in a genuine manner so we knew when we left we could call him for help, and most importantly that he emphasized the importance of never placing limitations on Cameron. He did not give us false hope about what abilities Cameron would attain in his life, but he did give us hope. When Dr. Shah told us "The day you say Cameron will never do something, he never will!" he provided us with a life philosophy that gave us the ability to get up each and every day and face the day with a sense of hope rather than a gloom and doom attitude. I also spoke about how important it is to treat a patient as a person and not just as a diagnosis/disability/illness. As an example I talked about an instance in which a physician first meeting Cam and I came into the exam room and stated "Oh this is our new patient with cerebral palsy" to which I quickly replied, no this is Cameron! I emphasized this point by sharing a phrase that I often use "Please do not label me, rather enable me to be everything that I can be!" I came up with this saying when preparing for a presentation for education majors at our local university.

Additionally, I shared information about Early Intervention services and the importance of obtaining services as early as possible. From our experiences, I was able to detail the support that EI provides to the entire family and how the entire process works from initial contact through evaluations and obtaining services. Angela, the EI parent liaison, also gave me some brochures to hand out and I did notice that every attendee took one. Cameron began therapy at only four months of age because we wanted to give him every opportunity to maximize the healthy areas of his brain.

Finally, I explained the role Tim and I play as Cameron's parents in helping to work with the medical professionals. We consider ourselves an equally important part of Cameron's team and so do each of his team members. I talked about setting expectations with a patient and/or patient's family so that everyone understands the role that they will play. I made sure that I asked each of Cam's team members how to best communicate with them. Would they prefer to be contacted via phone or fax when needing to set up referrals, as questions arose and prescription refills needed to be obtained? Likely, I explained what our expectations were and what would be helpful for us. I talked about needing to have time to ask my questions, needing to have support during those tough times when Cameron would plateau and most importantly needing reassurance from time to time so that we knew what we were doing for Cam was in his best interests. I am a doer so I asked each of his therapists to provide us with exercises to work on at home. To best accomplish this we dedicated the last 10 minutes of each therapy session to them showing me what we could work on at home until his next session. I asked for resources when they found them such as articles, support groups and books.

The final point that I emphasized about Cam's team was that ultimately Cameron is the one who has to work so hard and feel motivated to do so. I shared with the group how each member of Cam's team really makes Cameron the main focus of attention when they begin an appointment or therapy session by spending time talking to him and getting to know him. Since Cam is the one who is doing all of the hard work he needs to feel pride in his accomplishments and have a sense of control in the entire process. Yes, Tim and I are helping Cam by scheduling all of his appointments and following through with recommendations from his team but ultimately Cam is the key player and he deserves to be treated as such. Even though there are so many medical issues that Cam does face ultimately we also need to remember that this is a little boy who deserves to have the opportunity to experience what other little boys his age are experiencing and to share those experiences. By doing this Cam's team gets to really know Cameron and who he is since he is so much more than his diagnosis!

After my presentation, I showed the DVD montage I had made and answered some questions. Dr. Mangurten, the director of Pediatrics, then talked and explained to the residents how important my family's message is. Regardless of how much medical knowledge they have, without compassion and the skills to deliver difficult diagnoses the knowledge would not be quite so valuable. Dr. Shah then got up to talk and he said that he learned something very valuable during my presentation that had never occurred to him. He said as he sat and listened to me talk about the night he spent two hours with us and delivered the news to us he was surprised at how much of that conversation I remembered. It was amazing to hear how the words that he had spoke three years ago had such an impact and left such a lasting impression. He said that it reminded him too how important what is said really is.

After Dr. Shah spoke, I received a big round of applause and many people did stop to thank me for sharing our experience. Dr. Mangurten and Dr. Lundblad asked if I would be interested in speaking again and of course I said yes. To be honest that presentation was equally as important to Tim and I as it was for the residents and medical students. I feel like I finally have found a way to give back and to help make a bit of sense of all that happened to our family and specifically Cam and to hope that another family does not have to receive such hard news in the wrong manner like we did when Cam was just one week old and not yet a patient of Dr. Shah.

A few days after my presentation I sat down to write a letter to Drs. Shah, Mangurten and Lundblad thanking them for giving me the opportunity to present Cameron's Journey: A Story of Hope and Inspiration. Here is the letter I wrote them that captures my feelings and emotions that this experience gave me:

Dr. Shah, Dr. Mangurten and Dr. Lundblad,

I wanted to send a letter to thank each of you so much for giving me the opportunity to share Cameron's story on December 6th. Words cannot begin to explain how honored I felt to present at Advocate Lutheran General Hospital. As I was sharing Cameron's story and our family's journey with the residents and medical students in attendance, I was impressed by the degree of attentiveness each showed to me as they listened to me speak. After sharing Cameron's story and showing his video montage, the questions that were then asked also indicated to me that the importance of what I was sharing was not only noticed but that there was a sincere desire to learn more.

When I first decided to write the thank you letter to you, Dr. Shah, for giving us hope and helping us to realize the importance of providing Cameron with the support he needs to become everything that he can be back in July, I was so honored when you called me and told me you shared my letter with Dr. Mangurten. You recognized that I had a sincere desire to share Cameron's story with the hope of helping to educate people in the medical community about the impact the words that they speak to a patient or patient's family have on that patient's future. After speaking to you, Dr. Mangurten, about sharing Cameron's story with the residents at Lutheran General, I was also inspired to find ways to help parents in our community who are just beginning their journey into the world of special-needs parenting. From that moment on, I began to work on publicly sharing Cameron's story. In just five short months we have had articles written in the Northwest Herald, The Rock River Times as well as the Village Life of Huntley. Each person who reads Cameron's story is another person we are able to share a message of hope with and to help make a difference. We also created Cameron's Web site as another tool to reach members of our community.

December 6th was such an amazing experience for me. In the process of sharing our family's experience I found myself feeling an incredible amount of pride for our family and all that we have endured. Every day I watch Cameron in amazement and marvel at his will and determination to overcome each and every obstacle that he encounters. His ability to trust in others and his love for his medical team never ceases to amaze me. I am awed by our four and a half year-old daughter, Abby, and her ability to understand that the world is made up of people with all different abilities and that each person's life is one to be celebrated. I see her interact with children with special needs and her ability to see each child for who they are rather than what disability they have is an incredible gift that she has been given as a result of being Cam's sister. And I can honestly say that Tim and I have grown and changed. Our lives were filled with so much uncertainty three years ago and rather than face a lifetime filled with a doom and gloom attitude we were guided to embrace and enjoy each moment of Cam's and to never assume never. What a gift we were given by you, Dr. Shah, at a time when we were hearing such devastating medical news about our son.

Again, I want to thank each of you for recognizing the importance that hope plays in the life of a patient and their family and for allowing me to share that message with the residents and medical students of Advocate Lutheran General Hospital. Please know that I am always willing to share Cameron's story and help in any way that you feel would be beneficial.

Sincerely,
Becki Enck

Look at Dr. Cam and Dr. Abby in their scrubs!

A Video Project with Danielle Guerra

After presenting Cameron's Journey at Advocate Lutheran General Hospital I continued to write to area newspapers to share Cameron's story. Another reporter from the Northwest Herald wrote another story about Cameron and our family and this time the story made the front page! We received a call from a reporter/videographer named Danielle Guerra with the newspaper who asked if she could create a video documentary about Cameron to accompany that story and we agreed to meet at our area McDonald's. Danielle had so much fun watching Abby and Cameron playing and the video she made turned out great. She had so many great shots of Cameron climbing in the tunnels, talking with Abby, counting to ten, hugging my mom and she had interviewed me as well on the tape.

After meeting Danielle and seeing the beautiful video documentary she did of Cameron and our family, I decided to contact her to see if she would be interested in doing a freelance project with me. I wanted to create a video documentary of Cameron that I could share when I presented Cameron's story and I wanted it to be a video that could appeal to three main audiences. The three audiences would be medical professionals, education professionals and parents of children with special needs. I sent Danielle an e-mail to see if she did any freelance videography and after checking with her employer she e-mailed me back that yes, she definitely could and would be interested in meeting to talk about the project I had in mind. Danielle loved the ideas I had and immediately thought of some additional ideas as well.

From that first meeting we were both excited and we began the taping immediately. I contacted Dr. Shah and he agreed to participate in the video and we set up for Danielle to accompany us for an appointment with Dr. Shah. It was so fun because Danielle drove the thirty five miles with us to Advocate Lutheran General Hospital and Cam was talking and playing with her the entire time. He brought his play camera with to be just like Danielle and he made her laugh because she would say to him Cool Dude and he would say it back in the cutest little voice. He also tried to say Macaroni! Danielle said after the visit that Dr. Shah was exactly how she expected him to be based on how we had described what a caring and compassionate man he was.

Danielle and her boyfriend Ryan also joined us for Cameron's 4th birthday party at a local farm called Tom's Farm. Cam and Abby love to go to Tom's farm and so we had his party there. We went on a wagon ride into the field and each child was able to choose a pumpkin and gourds, then we played in the play area with hay bundles, an obstacle course and other fun things. The party ended with a birthday cake and presents in the party room. Danielle and Ryan had a lot of fun and said they had never sung Happy Birthday so many times at one party. Cameron had the kids singing to him out in the field, in the play area and then over and over again in the party room.

Danielle also came by to interview Tim and me separately for the video. She could not stop laughing when Tim wanted her to keep taping him—he said he gets very few chances at fame between Cam, Abby and I always being quoted in the papers so he wanted to make sure Danielle gave him plenty of "on-air" time! To finish up the video project Danielle decided to take home the videos we had taken of Cam as a baby to incorporate footage as well as some fun digital pictures that I had as well.

The process of creating this video with Danielle gave our family a chance to get to know Danielle and Ryan. They are both very generous people who very much care about the community in which they live and understand the importance of making a difference. They will both be walking in the breast cancer walk this summer, they attend various fundraising events and they have opened their hearts up and embraced Abby, Cameron, Tim and I. The beautiful video that I now have to share during presentations is a token of their generosity, care and compassion.

Danielle is also a freelance photographer and videographer and she can be reached at dguerraphoto@gmail.com.

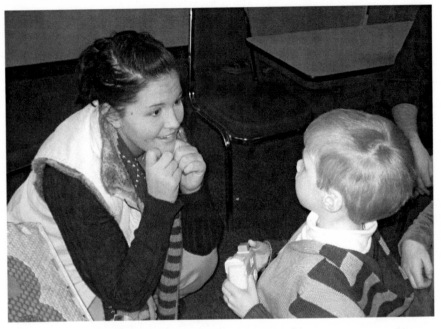

Danielle is listening to Cam talk about his camera.

Letters to Cameron

Some of the special people in Cameron's life have written letters to him and they agreed to have these letters shared in this book.

A letter from DaDa:

Dear Cameron,

Wow, what can I say, I cannot believe you are already 4-years-old. It only seems like yesterday we were waiting for you to enter our lives. I remember every moment on that day you were born. What excitement you brought, our second child was finally here and now Abby would have a little brother to boss around. A big sister at last, she was thrilled to see you and from that moment on a strong bond was made.

Over the past 4 years I have seen you change so much. I have seen you endure a lot of discomfort and pain and I have seen you fight every step of the way. You never gave up the fight and you were determined to do those things some people said you never would. You never gave up. I'm so proud of you.

Through the past 4 years I have seen you grow into a little boy; no more baby and no more toddler. A four year boy in many ways is like every other little boy with a devilish side. We were so proud the day you could walk, jump, and run. Little did we know you would also be walking on the kitchen table, jumping from the couch, and take Abby's things to antagonize her. And all the time you would have that sinister look in your eyes and a belly full of giggles as you would run away when we would chase after you. Yes, those little devilish horns are sure growing on your head. But what joy it is to be running after you.

You have been through so much and conquered so much in these first 4 years. I look forward to your future. I cannot wait to celebrate your continued accomplishments and to see you strive to fulfill your dreams and wishes. I will always be there by your side.

Love,

Dada

DaDa and Cam being silly.

A letter from Abby—Cameron's big sister, best friend and #1 supporter. Abby was five-years-old when she told me what to write to her little brother:

Dear Cam,

"Cam you are very special and you are so important because when you were a baby, I went to the hospital to see you. You invited me to your 4th birthday party and you play with me all of the time outside on the swing set. Cam, you are my best friend and I love you a lot! I love my Cameron."

Love, Abby

Abby decided to draw this special picture to include in the book.
She drew a picture of Cam watching her ride her scooter.

A letter from Me-Mom—Cameron's maternal grandmother:

Dear Cameron,

This is a special letter from me to you. When you were a new baby I helped mommy by taking care of you a few hours a day. During our visits I would sit and hold you the entire time, it was a very special time for me.

Now that you have become a big boy, Me-Mom always smiles to herself over all of the things you do. When I come over to see you, you are in the window waiting for me to come in and you get so excited to see me.

When you and Abby are playing, you come over to me for no reason at all and give me the biggest hugs ever. When we are walking down the stairs I always hold your hand and now you pull away and show me You Can Do It! It makes me happy to see you becoming so independent.

I love you Cameron, you will always be my little Mister!

Love,
Me-Mom xoxox

Cam with Me-Mom!

A letter from Aunt Sandy—Cameron's Great Aunt who was there when Cameron was placed on a ventilator at one week of age:

Dear Cameron,

As I am writing this letter to you, I can't believe you have just turned four-years-old! What a big boy you have become!

You have faced many challenges, and through it all you have shown everyone what hard work and determination can accomplish. We can all learn a lesson from you, Cam!

I hope you know what a great family you have. Your Mommy, DaDa, and Abby are so special. Our whole family is proud of you and loves you very much.

When you look at me with that mischievous twinkle in your eye and great big smile, you make my day. My wish for you is to keep smiling and always be happy. You are a sweet boy, Cam, and you have touched my heart in a special way.

Lots of Love,
Aunt Sandy

This picture was taken at Cam's 1st birthday party

A letter from Great Uncle Lee and Great Aunt Judie (my dad's brother and wife):

"CAM THE MAN"

Cameron Enck is an unbelievable young man with two very remarkable parents. Against all odds, this little guy has progressed way beyond anyone's expectations. One of Cam's main accomplishments has got to be his singing ability!!!!! He is very sure that he is one of the greatest, and you know what—he is.

Last Christmas, we had a Holiday gathering in which Cam found the fireplace area in the house that has a hearth that is elevated. This became "HIS" stage. Not for Christmas carols, but for his own rendition of "HAPPY BIRTHDAY", which I guess could really be called a Christmas Carol after all. Cam was on stage for quite awhile making sure we got the Happy Birthday message and he received the clapping he well deserved.

This will always be one of those moments in time which stays in your heart forever and when I think about Cam, his stage debut, and the happiness we all felt, I know I must get this little smile on my face. I also know that when Cam is 12 or so, he won't want us to talk about it.

We love you Cam,
Great Uncle Lee and Great Aunt Judie

A photo that makes Great Aunt Judie and Great Uncle Lee laugh!

A letter from Amy—a friend of our family:

Hello Cam!

I just wanted to tell you about the first day we met. Your sister Abby and my Emma were in the same class in school together. Both your Mom and I were having a hard time with them starting school. When we came to pick the girls up and you were in your stroller, you looked up at me with your big blue eyes and smiled. I fell in love with you at that very moment. I barely knew your Mom or Abby but I knew I melted when you smiled at me. I knew we would become good friends and have good times as well as helping each other out through the bad times.

In the past few years of getting to know you and your beautiful family, I have found you to be part of my family. I have watched you grow and change before my very eyes. A little boy afraid of the jungle gym set now runs all over with the big kids. A little boy who would hum the Jeopardy song is now talking up a storm.

I look forward to seeing you grow and change more and more every day!

Keep smiling! I love you!

Amy

Amy brought Cam a birthday present. Here she is with two of her four children, Emma and Sarah, along with Abby and Cam.

A letter from Leigh Anne—a friend of our family:

Dear Cam,

It has been my pleasure to watch you grow and change over the past year and a half. You are a very fun and sweet little boy with an amazing amount of energy. Your smile always brightens my day and warms my heart. Your charisma and continually improving abilities never cease to amaze me. I have learned a lot through your challenges and many triumphs. You have touched my heart and made an impact in my life as well as that of Mr. Dean and Devan, Dustin, and Kayleigh. Devan and Dustin have really enjoyed all of our play dates and special outings together. We already have many precious memories of our times with you, Abby, your Mommy, DaDa, and Me-Mom. We have been very blessed by the friendship of your family. We look forward to many more years of friendship and special times together and the opportunity to continue to watch you grow and prosper.

Thank you for allowing us to be part of your village. You are an amazing little boy and I know you will accomplish great things in your life. Continue to live your life following the very important principles that your parents have relied on and have taught you. Never say never and always have hope and faith.

With love,
Your friend Miss Leigh Anne

Cam loves to sit on Miss Leigh Anne's lap when
she is over and he loves to play with her too!

A letter from Angela—a friend of our family and the parent liaison for Early Intervention:

Dear Cameron,

I have been blessed to know you and your family since shortly after you were born. I don't think you will ever fully understand the kind of positive impact you have made on all those around you.

There was a time when some people were willing to give up hope on you, but never your family. Instead they kept looking until they found a group of people ready to fight alongside of them for you. I remember talking with your mom when you were still a baby and she was feeling very sad and unsure about the future. Within a very short amount of time, she has been able to find happiness and use her experiences with you to help so many other people. Your journey along with your family is inspiring. As I write this, you have no idea what is happening around you and how many lives you are touching. I can't wait until you are old enough to read this and try to grasp your place in this world.

Many people are always in search of a way to make a place for themselves in the world, you have done that from birth, without even trying. You work hard every day, you endure pain and frustrations that we will never understand, and you do all this without complaining. Unfortunately, those of us without the challenges you face daily find ridiculous reasons to complain about nonsense things, while you just keep working through it. We could all learn more than a few lessons from you.

I truly believe everything happens for a reason even though those reasons may not be known to us. Your family has been blessed by you, and I think it is obvious that you have also been blessed by them. I can only imagine what the future holds for you and all those your life touches. You have a lot of work ahead of you and I am confident that with the support and positive message your family is spreading you will be impacting lives for a long time to come. I look forward to watching God work through you to change lives; it is a beautiful thing to witness.

May God Bless You Always,
Angela Krambeer

Angela and I at a fundraiser for Options & Advocacy (Early Intervention).

A letter from Danielle—a friend of our family who also created a video of Cameron:

> When I had first heard about Cameron's story, I was in the newsroom. A reporter told me about this story she had written about a little boy and his family's fight to make sure that no other family had to endure what they went through. I asked questions about the family, the little boy named Cameron and their situation.
>
> I decided that capturing this story on video would make a nice addition to the story in the newspaper so people could see Cameron interact and play. I met Becki, Cameron, Abby and "Me-Mom" at the local McDonalds, where they came to play regularly after Cameron's rehab. Looking around, I couldn't have told you who Cameron was, I didn't see anyone with a disability. I imagined, maybe a walker or a wheelchair from the diagnosis I had heard. But there was Cameron, 3-years-old at the time, a little ball of energy in his bright red shirt, blowing kisses to all the workers. I couldn't help but laugh to myself and blow him a kiss back.
>
> Hearing Becki's story about the initial grim diagnosis that they were given made me wonder how a doctor could take advantage of such a young life. I could see the hurt on Becki's face as she described how everything unfolded. Some people would have just given up, threw their hands up and said that's it. But not the Enck family. They have turned devastating into hopeful with the support of a large caring medical staff and plenty of family, friends, and teachers along the way.
>
> I'm amazed, every time I see Cam. Whether I drop by just to see them, go to Tom's Farm for his birthday, or have him take a grand tour of the fire house that my boyfriend Ryan works at, I'm amazed how much growth this little boy has made in just one year. Cam and his family have proven those original doctors wrong. We're proud of you Cam, cool dude, keep up the good work buddy!
>
> Danielle Guerra

Cameron and Abby with Danielle and Ryan at the Woodstock Fire Station #2.

A letter from Miss Kim—Cam's speech therapist during his first year of preschool in District #47 and a friend to our family:

Dear Cam,

I miss working with you in speech, and I want you to know how much I enjoyed our therapy sessions together! You made such awesome progress in only one year, and you worked so diligently to meet your goals.

When you first started the program at the Early Childhood Center, in District 47 Schools (Crystal Lake, IL), you were three-years-old; you communicated only with vowel sounds, a few signs, and a few single words. You enjoyed looking at short books, and running around and climbing on toys. Your attention span for an activity was less than a minute. At snack time, you didn't like to sit in your chair, you packed your mouth as fast as possible with food, and you didn't like to "wait." You were intensely focused on music, the boom box, and any toy that made sound. Nevertheless, you were a child with many special gifts.

You lit up a room when you ran into it. Your smile could melt any mother's heart, and your positive spirit and enthusiasm for life were inspirational to me. I knew that you had the ability to gain the tools that you needed to communicate more effectively.

You worked so hard! We started with sign language as sign language often facilitated verbal speech. You quickly picked up signs such as "I want more," "help," "open," "up," etc. We gave all of your classmates name signs, and constructed a sign scrapbook with each of their pictures and their names. Your family added their pictures to your scrapbook, and you told me about your adorable sister Abby and your Me-Mom. You loved to express the words, "I did it!" when you accomplished a goal. A *Cheap Talk* was used at snack as an aide in sequencing pictures to make your wants and needs known.

Phonological goals were worked on through <u>Silly Noisy Stories,</u> and through drills, games, music, and play. Cued speech was used to help you visually sequence sounds. We played with play dough, and worked on requesting, regulating others' behavior, asking for help, and taking turns.

Before long, you were chaining several words in sign, and as the signs became too cumbersome, you started to substitute words! By the end of the year, you were verbally chaining 5-6 word sentences, sitting for extended periods of time, attending to lengthy stories, eating with one bite at a time at snack, and requesting help and objects spontaneously.

There were times during the year that you and your family were tested with trying circumstances. When you were hospitalized for a week, Dr. Shah at Advocate Lutheran General worked tirelessly with your family to regulate your little body with the medicines that it needed. Your sister supported you with her presence, her patience and her love. Your mom and dad were relentless in their quest to find the best possible solutions to your health and communication needs, and to advocate for you as a patient. Cam, you were surrounded by love and hope and the support of people who believed in you. And through this entire ordeal, you were a trooper!

I have always believed that God puts special people in our lives to give us insight into ourselves. I think that God blessed me with the opportunity to work with you so that I could learn about exceeding one's limitations. You taught me to be a better speech-language pathologist, and you demonstrated through your enthusiasm and love of life, the excellence that can come with hard work. You and your family will always be inspirational to me. Thank you, Cam, for allowing me to be part of your world, and for being one of my best teachers.

With love to you and your family,
Miss Kim

Miss Kim with Abby and Cam on the last day of Cam's first year of preschool.

A letter from Jamie—Cameron's developmental therapist for two years:

Dear Cameron,

My name is Jamie Mills, and I was your Developmental Therapist for almost two whole years! I wanted to take some time to write you a letter about all the wonderful times we had together in our therapy sessions. I have so many fond memories of you, but I am going to pick out a few that really stick out in my mind. I am hoping that you can look back at this letter when you are all grown up, and see just how many goals and milestones you accomplished when you were a little boy. I also want you to appreciate all the love, encouragement, understanding, compassion, and opportunities your family gave to you, when at times they were told that you would not be able to do many of the things that a child without Cerebral Palsy could do. They always made sure to give you every opportunity to grow and reach your highest potential.

When I initially started seeing you, walking was still a challenge for you. You did show me how you could walk by holding on to a chair or your Mommy's hand, but you were a little scared to take that first step by yourself. You also did not know how to play with toys appropriately. You could bang them together, put them in your mouth, and throw them, but had a hard time engaging in constructive play activities. It was difficult for you to stack blocks, place the rings on the post, and complete simple puzzles. You also had a very short attention span, which made it hard for you to sit still for long periods of time.

As time progressed.... You learned how to do so many wonderful things. You were always happy to see me and greeted me with a great big smile. I will never forget how you liked to look at and touch my dark brown hair. You also learned how to walk and soon started to run all over the house. You became very interested in a wide variety of toys and also learned how to communicate your wants and needs using sign language and words. I was so proud of how you could match your shapes, color with crayons, stack the blocks, and make animal sounds. You were also my little helper and learned how to clean up after you were done playing with a toy. The cutest thing was when you would say "sorry" after you did something you weren't supposed to do, like throw the toys across the room. Finally, you and your family found a place in my heart, and I will never forget all the memories that we created together.

I know that you are going to do amazing things as you get older and I hope that all your dreams and wishes come true. I look forward to hearing all about them, so please make sure to keep in touch in the future.

Best of Luck and Warmest Regards,
Jamie Mills, Developmental Therapist

Cameron loved playing with Jamie. As he got older, Jamie would have Cam sit in his booster seat and buckle him in or else he would be running all around the house!

A letter from Heather—Cameron's home speech therapist during the summer of 2006:

Dear Cameron,

I just wanted to write you a little note to tell you how much I enjoyed working with you and your family. Just seeing your smile could always brighten my day! We had so much fun playing with blocks, puzzles, books, and of course, your favorite, music. Abby was always there to help you learn and grow. I know you will continue to succeed with the help of dedicated teachers, therapists, doctors, and your wonderful family. Always remember to work hard and play hard! I wish you the very best for what is to come and look forward to your continued achievement.
Your Friend,
Miss Heather

Cameron loved playing with Miss Heather!

Our Family Today

After I completed writing this book and edits were performed, I realized that there is still so much to tell about our family and who we are today. I would like to share some updates with you about each of us at the time of publication of this book.

Cameron is now four-and-a-half-years-old and completing his second year of preschool. Cameron has grown so much this year in preschool. He was an independent preschooler this year, no longer requiring a one-on-one aide. Although he missed Miss Carolyn, he still would see her some mornings going into school and he always had a beautiful smile for her. Cam shared more details about preschool with us this year. He would talk about the different children and what he had done in school. Each project he brought home he would proudly show us and say "I made this!" Cameron's vocabulary grew by leaps and bounds and there were days that we were hearing multiple new words, words that sometimes we did not even know that he knew. He continued to enjoy learning new songs and would sing them at home to us. Next year he will attend the afternoon session of the preschool program since he will not turn five until mid September.

At home, Cameron still struggles with impulse control issues although we are finding that he is starting to recognize when his frustration level is reaching a boiling point and sometimes he can calm himself down. He is also able to better verbalize his needs and wants which is also helping to alleviate some frustration on all of our parts.

Cameron participates in some extracurricular activities through the Northern Illinois Special Recreation Association (NISRA) and really looks forward to his classes. On Saturdays, he attends Tots of Fun which is a drop-off program where Cameron spends two and a half hours in class. He loves all of the children and knows each staff member. They do arts and crafts, sing songs, play outside when the weather permits and have some free play time too. He also gets to bring his lunch and eat with his friends. Although the first two weeks that he attended he was concerned about whether we were coming back to pick him up he is now confident that Mommy, DaDa and Abby are coming back and so he really enjoys every minute of his class. While Cam is at his class, Tim, Abby and I get to spend some time together. Each week we let Abby pick different activities to do with just Mommy and DaDa and she loves it. Sometimes she will pick to go to the library, a park, Chuck E. Cheese or the bookstore. Each Saturday she always starts our time together by choosing to go to a bagel shop in Crystal Lake that we love. We all cherish our special time together.

Cameron's social skills are really progressing. He is initiating play time with Abby often and really enjoys when we have special play dates with friends. Cameron loves to play with his jungle animals, ride his scooter and he loves to play doctor. Abby and Cam have a medical cart and they each have medical bags with play equipment so Tim and I usually get our check-ups daily. Cam is still very interested in Abby's toys and especially her American Girl Dolls Kit and Nikki, which occasionally Abby will let him hold. Tim and I just laugh because he will sit on her bed and just hold her dolls for as long as she will let him. Of course temptation always gets the best of him and when he starts to touch their hair Abby promptly takes her dolls away from him. She is very particular about her special dolls and she does not want them to have their hair pulled like she has so often had done to her. Cam is also very interested in books. Abby is gaining more and more confidence in her reading abilities and now will sit down with Cam to read him a book. He will sit by her the entire time and just smile. I know he is very proud of his big sister. And puzzles are also a favorite of Cam's as well. He has over 15 wooden puzzles and each are stored in a puzzle bag with a picture of the completed puzzle. He will take out a puzzle, dump all the pieces and then he turns all of the pieces upside down before he will start rebuilding the puzzle. He has gotten very good at the puzzles and very rarely will he get frustrated while working on them.

Cam absolutely loves my mom, Me-Mom, and every time he sees her he greets her with a five minute long hug. It is so funny because even if he saw her a few hours earlier when he sees her again he reacts with the same excitement of seeing her again. Of course it certainly melts his Me-Mom's heart. He also loves when he sees my brother Scott. He will start yelling Uncle Scott, Uncle Scott and he always tries to grab Scott's glasses. If Scott is helping Tim with an electrical project (he is an electrician), Cam is right there at the bottom of the ladder anxiously awaiting his turn to climb. Scott always laughs because Cam has no fear and he has made it to the top of the ladder quite a few times.

Cameron did re-enter physical therapy as well. Luckily he is able to see Dolores, his original physical therapist. We started to notice that Cam was losing some strength on his right side and he was really pulling up his right arm as he performed any activity. He also is still not pedaling a tricycle or kicking a ball. So Dolores is working with Cameron weekly to help him to gain strength and master the skills he is delayed in performing.

We also learned that Cameron's food allergies have worsened. He went through re-testing and his peanut allergy has now progressed to the highest level possible, so it is now a level six, whereas three years ago it was a level four. Needless to say we were disappointed to learn this because we had hoped his allergy would have subsided and certainly did not expect to hear that it had worsened.

In summary, Cam is a happy four-and-a-half-year-old toddler who absolutely loves his big sister Abby and daily amazes us with all of his physical abilities, his communication skills and his determination to work so hard to be the best he can be!

Cam looks so happy holding Kit and Nikki

Abby is now six-years-old and completing Kindergarten. She absolutely loved her year in school and we have watched her emerge as a very confident and caring little girl who started the school year with a lot of separation anxiety and doubts. Abby had one of the most caring teachers, Mrs. Miller, who has really embraced our family and understands the challenges that Abby faced as a young toddler when her brother was born and so very sick. Mrs. Miller gave Abby the encouragement she needed and also the time she needed to gain confidence in herself. It took a few months of daily praise and positive encouragement for Abby to begin to raise her hand in class and answer questions. Once she started, there was no stopping her. Mrs. Miller also helped me to realize that the guilt that I sometimes feel about having left Abby when she was so young and Cameron was sick is something that I need to let go of. Abby knows that I love her and that I have been and will always be there for her. She also understands that sometimes I need to be with Cameron at the hospital. Mrs. Miller told me that Abby talks daily about the fun things we do together and how much she cherishes the time we spend together.

Abby gained confidence to also join two extracurricular activities in the Winter/Spring and really felt pride in herself. At school, she attended a weekly art class called Young Rembrandts that met at the end of the day. She knew no one when she signed up to attend and ending up really enjoying meeting some new friends. Mrs. Miller would stop by and peek in the room each week and Abby really enjoyed that. She also loved that her art projects were hung in the gym and all of her classmates would see what she had done on Thursdays during gym class. Abby also signed up for a ballet/tap class with her friend Emily and they had a blast at their weekly dance class. It was fun to watch Abby participate in some extra activities and know that she was truly enjoying them. She seemed to be able to let herself enjoy her class without worrying about whether or not I would return to pick her up.

Abby's favorite thing to play is school and she loves when Tim, Cam or I sit with her as a student. She will run her classroom just as Mrs. Miller runs Kindergarten. It is so fun to watch her imagination at work and to also see a true love for learning and for teaching others emerging. When we ask Abby what she thinks she wants to be when she grows up she will tell us a special education teacher. I have to say that it will not surprise me if that is what she chooses and if so, I know she will be a phenomenal teacher.

Abby also loves to play with her American Girl dolls. She keeps them in her room because she does not want Cam to have unsupervised access to them. She has many different clothes as well as furniture pieces for them so she spends quite a bit of time playing with them. Abby is also very creative and daily will make beautiful pictures, cards and other art projects for us. She loves to start her morning coloring, and using scissors and glue are a particular favorite. She is cautious to keep her supplies away from Cam though!

The upcoming school year will bring some changes for Abby. Kindergarten in our school district was half day so Abby would be home for lunch and the afternoon with Cam and I. First grade is a full school day so she will be bringing her lunch with her and away for several more hours. She is excited though. As the end of Kindergarten approaches, Abby keeps telling me that she would like to stay at school longer so I think that the transition to first grade will not be too difficult.

In summary, Abby is a six-year-old independent girl who is one of the most caring and compassionate people Tim and I have ever met. Abby continues to support Cameron and never hesitates to help him to accomplish something he is struggling with. She continues to tell us that he is her best friend and her actions certainly support her words. Daily she makes us beam with pride, a pride that words cannot begin to describe.

Abby with Mrs. Miller

Tim and I are slowly but surely learning to slow down and relax. We are focused on enjoying the moments rather than worrying about the tomorrows. It is hard to do and there are still days where one of us will start to slip but then the other points it out. We are also realizing that we both do need some personal time and so we plan days that each of us gets to take a break and go do something just for us. Sometimes it might mean that we go grab a bite to eat alone or go and hang out at the bookstore. It is our choice. When the weather is nice, Tim will go golfing, something he really enjoys doing and did not get to do very much the first few years of Cam's life. I enjoy writing and often will go to a coffee shop and write. I also love getting together with other moms and we will go shopping or for a bite to eat.

In terms of sharing our journey over the past four years we have some common goals. We are committed to supporting other parents of children with special needs, to educating the medical community on how to deliver a devastating diagnosis with care and compassion as well as to raise awareness among society in general about the importance of never placing limitations on a person with a disability.

We talk often of some day taking a vacation, just the two of us, and reminisce about our wedding and honeymoon in Maui. Then we laugh and say well maybe for our twenty-fifth anniversary we will make it back to Maui.

We have also realized that even though both of us have had very different ways of dealing with the many sad moments that we encountered over the past four years, it did not mean that we do not care to the same extent. We just have different ways of expressing our emotions and we are learning to respect those differences.

When Tim and I get an opportunity to go out to dinner or a show together, we inevitably find ourselves talking all about Abby and Cameron. And even though we only will leave them for two to three hours with my mom, we find that we miss them when we are away from them and we hurry back home to see them.

Many days I still question myself. I ask myself how I can do this. How can I trust that I will know what Cameron needs and how to go about giving him all of the opportunities that will help him to become the best he can be? I had no prior experience with children with special needs until I had Cameron. Until I had Cam, I had never met someone with cerebral palsy. I ask so many questions of Cameron's medical team, I search the Internet for information and I talk to other parents of children with special needs. And yet it still does not feel like enough. I have never had to learn something so important. In college and in graduate school I excelled. I knew exactly was expected of me and I went above and beyond those expectations. I sought out additional information and really enjoyed learning each and every fact that I could. But this is different. This is not a matter of learning material to get a good grade on a test or to graduate top of my class so that I can land that ideal job. This is my son and his life. What I do will determine his future. And I have to be honest, that is scary.

Earlier I talked about how God chose us to be Cameron's parents and how he knew that I would have the strength to provide Cameron with all of the medical interventions he would need while also providing him with a mother's love that he would need. I find myself questioning my abilities at times of change for Cameron, especially when he has reached a big milestone and then we need to work toward the next milestone. I tend to not realize how strong of a person I am sometimes. I have endured a lot these past few years. I was able to stay on hospital bed rest for thirty-seven days while I awaited the premature arrival of my daughter Abby. Because of that, Abby was born six, rather than eleven, weeks prematurely and has no lasting effects of her prematurity. And I have endured watching my son being placed on a ventilator, being told that we made the wrong decision and that he would have no functionality and ultimately learning that Cameron has cerebral palsy. I have learned that our son's life should be celebrated and I watch him daily in amazement and think about all that he will become. I am a strong woman and most importantly I am a mother who has been given two extraordinary gifts from God. And my two gifts are named Abby and Cameron. I thank God every day that I was chosen to be their mom!

Abby and Cameron
May 2008

THE END

Special Thanks

There are so many people that I would like to thank for all of their love and support over the past few years. I have described each person and the gift that they have given to us and hope you will enjoy reading about each one.

Tim: On our wedding invitations we chose the saying "I love you not only for who you are but for what I am when I am with you." Thank you for being the most amazing Dad. Because of you, I am the mom that I am. You have stood by my side during some very sad moments and never once did I doubt that you would not be there. I feel so blessed to be your wife and the mother of your children. Every day I watch you with our children and I am so thankful that we are a family. Together we can!

Abby: Words cannot begin to express the pride that Mommy and DaDa feel about you. You have showed us the power of unconditional love and you provide Cameron with the inspiration he needs to be all that he can be. You have patiently waited for him to achieve each of his milestones and have celebrated each victory with him. We love you with all of our heart and you are the most amazing big sister any brother could ever hope for!

Cameron: Cameron you are my amazing little boy who has taught me what is really important in life. I love being your mom and I absolutely love watching your whirlwind of activity all day long. Although I literally collapse into bed exhausted from chasing you each day, I would not want it any other way!

Aunt Sandy: You were with me when I needed someone the most. I would have never thought I could survive watching my son being placed on a ventilator and waiting for Tim to arrive. You were my strength and courage. Your support did not end when Cameron was stable. It has continued through countless e-mails and talks. The joy I see in your eyes when you see Cameron is such a gift not only to Cam but to me.

Dr. Mangurten and all of the staff at Advocate Lutheran General Hospital in Park Ridge, Illinois: Each and every one of you have provided Cameron and our family with the support we have needed since Cameron was just seven weeks of age. You have celebrated with us as we have watched Cameron accomplish each of his milestones, and you have supported us as we have cried through many of the obstacles he has faced. You have made it so that Cameron absolutely loves to go to the hospital! We thank each and every one of you for your commitment to providing the highest level of patient-centered care to our son and to our family!

Dr. Kaufman (Pediatrician) and staff of Pediatric Associates of Barrington: You have demonstrated a sincere commitment to helping Cameron become all that he can be. You have made it so that he absolutely loves to go to the doctor! You have answered the countless questions that we have had, provided advice at times of desperation and celebrated Cameron's reaching of milestones with us. Never once have you made us doubt or question our parenting abilities. Thank you for all of your support and patience!

Dolores (Physical Therapist): Through your encouragement, you gave us the joy of seeing our son walk, run and jump. When needed you were able to be tough and push Cameron to his limits, despite his many tears. And yet you were soft enough to provide me with a much needed shoulder to cry on.

Robin (Occupational Therapist): Through your patience, you have given us the joy of watching our son play with toys, write with crayons and explore the world around him. You provided him with a sense of confidence he needed to venture out and try new experiences. And yet you provided me with the security I needed in my abilities to let Cameron go and explore his world.

Dana (Speech Therapist): Through your determination, you have given us the joy of hearing our son say Hi DaDa, Hi Mommy, and other words. You provided Cameron with the praise he needed to express himself through signs and spoken words. And yet you provided me with the knowledge of language development to encourage signing first and trust that spoken words would follow—and they are!

Donna (Therapy Center): Through the sad and the happy times you let me be me. Never once did you tell me not to feel a certain way—you let me feel how I was feeling and for that I thank you tremendously. You provided me a safe place to share my greatest fears and my greatest joys. Thank you for making both of my children feel so incredibly special and important—you have been a true gift to our family!

Jamie (Developmental Therapist): Through your endless energy, you have given us the joy of hearing our son laugh and squeal with excitement during play. You have provided Cameron with the silliness he needed in his often too serious world. And yet you provided me with the seriousness I needed as I shared my frustrations and sorrows with you.

Heather (Home Speech Therapist): Through your hard work, you have given us the joy of hearing our son combine multiple words together. You have showed us how to prompt Cameron for multiple signs and word combinations so that we can better understand his needs and wants. We are amazed at Cameron's ability to tell us "I want.... ." You fulfilled your commitment to providing Cameron with the last 2 months of his home speech therapy and you did it with an unbelievable amount of energy, enthusiasm and professionalism.

Katie (EI Service Coordinator): Your coordination of all of Cameron's services as well as the emotional support that you provided me made these past four years for Cameron and our family so miraculous. You helped to arrange the services that have provided us with the joy of seeing our son walk, run, jump, play, laugh, sign and talk. The efforts that you put into making the Early Intervention process so smooth must have been endless.

Angela (EI Parent Liaison): You have taught me to appreciate the beauty of God's plan. You were the first person I expressed my fears to about being a parent to a child with special needs and your wisdom, openness and honesty opened my eyes and my heart to accepting that although our family was different than what I expected it to be, it is so much more than what I could have ever hoped and wished for. Our friendship is one that I cherish. Thank you for being my friend!

Danielle Guerra (Videographer, Photographer, and Friend) and Ryan Mains (Firefighter and Friend): You have captured the wonderment of Cameron on video for the world to see and to learn from. We have enjoyed watching both of you smile and laugh as you have watched our silly little boy. The admiration both of you have for Cameron and Abby is a gift you have given to us that we will forever cherish. Danielle is a freelance photographer and videographer and can be reached at dguerraphoto@gmail.com.

Andi Andree (Vocational Instructor in Sycamore, IL, Instructor at NIU, and Friend): Through your support and encouragement, you have allowed me to share Cameron's story with your education students at NIU. After each presentation, your students have given me the gift of sharing their thoughts and feelings in reaction papers they have written about my presentation and about children with special needs. I will forever cherish all of the thoughts that your students have chosen to share with me. You have also helped me so much by patiently answering all of my questions about how to best help Abby at times that we face acceptance issues. Thank you for your gift of friendship!

Julie Samuelson and Kim Hall (The Patient-Centered Care Institute): Through your encouragement, I am able to raise awareness about the importance of patient-centered care by sharing Cameron's Journey with health care professionals. Both of you have embraced our family and have helped us to meet other families as well as many health care professionals that share our passion to make a difference.

District #47 Crystal Lake Early Childhood Education Staff: Through your patience and dedication you have made Cameron a confident preschooler who loves going to school each and every day. You have encouraged him to try new things in a safe, loving and caring environment. After just two years, Cameron's communication and social skills have improved tremendously. It is incredible to see how Cameron feels about himself each day as he walks out of school and tells me "I did it!" Thank you for all that you do for Cameron and all of the children in our community.

Mrs. Miller (District #47 Kindergarten Teacher): Through your patience, encouragement and support you have given us the gift of watching Abby emerge as a confident soon to be first-grader who is now able to venture out and try new things. We have watched a true love for learning develop in Abby that will be a gift she will carry not only with her for a lifetime but a gift she will share with others as well. Thank you from the bottom of our hearts for the gifts you have given to Abby and our family.

Shannon Curcio (Photographer): Through your beautiful beach photos you have given our family the gift of forever seeing Cameron's smile and mischievous spirit. Your photos serve as a reminder that we worked together as a family to help make Cam everything that he can be. Thank you for your generous gift of your time and talents. Shannon is a freelance photographer and her beautiful work can be found on www.curciophoto.com.

Michael and Jessica Knight (Web Site Developers): Through the sharing of your talents you have given the world a way to see our son. Your technical knowledge of Web site development and your generous gift of your time and talents will forever capture each and every person's heart when they access www.cameronsjourney.com.

Family and Friends: You have walked with us through this journey. From phone calls to e-mails to visits you have cared about our family and helped to sustain our hope during those very rough times. You have also allowed us to share all of Cameron's accomplishments with you—making them even more special! Thank you, thank you each and every one of you!

About the Author

Becki Enck is the proud mother of Abby and Cameron. She is married to her husband Tim for nine years now and together they are helping each other to be the best that they can be! "Walking Hand in Hand with Cameron, Together We Can!" One Family's Journey with Cerebral Palsy is her first published book and she is excited to be sharing her family's journey of hope and inspiration with you.

Becki credits her husband Tim for helping her to become a published author. Tim was the one who encouraged her to follow through on writing this book one evening when she jokingly stated that she should write a book. Tim would encourage Becki to go out and write when he would get home from work, and as you can see Becki did just that, despite many temptations to just go out shopping during all of that free time!

Becki holds a Bachelor of Science Degree in Psychology from the University of Illinois in Champaign, IL and a Master's Degree of Public Health from Northern Illinois University in DeKalb, IL. The Enck family completed a patient narrative video, Cameron: A Child with Cerebral Palsy, in conjunction with the Center for Communication in Medicine at Northwestern University's Feinberg School of Medicine in 2007 that is used as an educational tool for medical students. The Enck family voluntarily participated in the creation of this video and gained an immeasurable amount of personal satisfaction from their participation which they have found to be priceless!

Becki is a speaker on the topics of Communication in Medicine as well as Disability Awareness. She has presented at the 2008 Accreditation Council for Graduate Medical Education's (ACGME) Annual Conference (February 2008), the NRC/Picker Institute's 14th Annual Symposium (September 2008), the Northwest and the Northern Illinois Special Recreation Association's (NWSRA and NISRA) annual staff orientations (2007) as well as to several classes of education majors at Northern Illinois University.

Becki, Tim, Abby and Cameron live in Crystal Lake, Illinois, a northwest suburb of Chicago.

Additional Resources

I Have Learned

I have learned so many important things these past four years about myself and about life. Some of the things I have learned include:

1. The love you feel for your child is the most intense type of love you can ever experience. When people say they would give their life for their child, they are being honest. I would do anything to protect both of my children.

2. Life is hard. No matter how many hard times you have had it does not make you exempt from more. And sometimes, when it rains it really does pour. If you do not give up, you will become a stronger person in the end. I am so much stronger than I ever thought.

3. No matter how hard we try we cannot protect our children from everything around them. I could not protect Cameron from contracting suspected meningitis, from suffering extensive brain damage, from developing severe food allergies and asthma. I have learned that even I cannot protect my children from everything.

4. For so long I looked to others to make me feel good about myself. I had unrealistic expectations and as result spent four years feeling so angry about the things this person did or that person did not do. Not only was this draining my energy but it was also blocking my ability to cherish all of the supportive people in our lives. Today I can say that I am working on focusing on all of the great people we have in our lives, because we are truly blessed and thankful for them!

5. Your child is worth fighting for. You are your child's best advocate. When faced with opposition, stay focused and persistent and never take NO for an answer. The doctors and therapists that you select to be a part of your child's medical team are just that—they are part of a team. All members of

the team need to work together to help your child become everything that they can be. If changes in the team need to be made then make them. In the end a team is only as strong as its weakest link, so pick all strong links because your child's life and future are too important.

6. It is important to stop and appreciate each moment you have with your child. Life is very unpredictable and you never know what tomorrow might bring. Stop and enjoy today!

7. It is important to ask for help from others. During Cameron's first year I tried to be superwoman and finally I realized I could not do it all. You are not a weak person if you ask for help. Rather you are a strong person for recognizing your limitations.

8. It is okay to feel angry that your child got sick or has challenges. Anger is a normal emotion and you are entitled to feel it. It is also okay to let go of that anger and celebrate your child's life, even if it is a very different life than you ever imagined. Every child's life deserves to be celebrated.

9. Sometimes people fear what they do not know or do not understand. Your child can teach others so many important lessons. Share their stories and help make a difference!

10. God did not make a mistake when he gave us a child with special needs. He recognized that Tim and I would be great parents for Cameron and chose us for this very important role. God knew that we would walk hand in hand with Cameron during this amazing journey of life. He chose us because he knew we would provide Cameron with the unconditional love and support he would need to become everything that he could be. How incredibly honored we feel to be chosen!

10 Things Medical Professionals Should Never Say

These ten items are based on actual things that medical professionals have said to us throughout Cameron's journey that we have found to be inappropriate and unacceptable. We also chose not to accept these statements and chose other medical professionals to be a part of Cameron's team. After all a team is only as strong as its' weakest link and we need the weakest link to be extremely strong. Our goal is to help our child become everything that he can be and with support and encouragement we can be successful in achieving that goal.

1. **Your child will have no brain functionality "IF" he/she survives.**

   No one can predict this. Despite significant brain damage, the healthy areas of a child's brain can be maximized through interventions such as physical therapy, speech therapy, occupational therapy and developmental therapy.

2. **I do not know what the hell the problem is.**

   If a physician does not know what is wrong with a child, it is acceptable to tell the parents in a professional manner. However, the physician needs to follow through by either finding possible explanations for the problem or referring the family to another medical professional who has specialized training to determine the problem.

3. **Oh, this is the patient with cerebral palsy!**

   Please do not ever refer to a patient as their disability. Each patient is a unique individual who has a name. The medical issue they suffer from does not define them as a person.

4. **The therapies you are receiving for your son are a waste of time and money. He is going to be who he is regardless of the intervention choices you make.**

   Research has proven that therapeutic interventions as early as possible in a child's life are beneficial in that they help to maximize the healthy areas of the brain to help compensate for the areas that have been permanently damaged.

5. **You need to accept that there are going to be many things your child will not be able to do, such as have a lucrative career, live on his own or attend college.**

   No one can predict a child's future. With the right encouragement and support, a family can provide their child with every opportunity to become all that they can be, whatever that is.

6. **Because your child has extensive brain damage his functionality will be extensively impaired.**

   There is no correlation with the amount of brain damage a child suffers and their level of functionality achieved. A child can suffer extensive brain damage such as Cam and present very well and a child can suffer minimal brain damage with less functional abilities.

7. **You need to forget about the past and not worry so much as new medical issues arise.**

   As a parent it is not possible to completely eliminate all of the feelings you have experienced and continue to experience as a result of having a child with an extensive medical background. You can encourage me to share my feelings and worries about what has happened so that I can move forward with my ability to handle each new medical crisis with a fresh perspective.

8. **Your child is not making enough progress to warrant additional therapy sessions.**

   As a child receives care for their medical condition there will be times that they may plateau in their progress. However, just because a child plateaus it does not indicate or warrant denying that child from receiving additional services, particularly when this determination is made based on paper and not actually seeing a child and how far they have progressed.

9. **Referring to a parent as "Mom" or "Dad" in a condescending manner.**

   I am Cameron's mom and Tim is Cameron's dad and you may call us Mom, Dad, Becki, Tim or Mr. and Mrs. Enck. The only thing that we ask is that it is not done in a demeaning manner. We always address you in a respectful manner, we ask that you address us with respect as well.

10. **I am the medical professional and I know best.**

    A parent's opinion and observations of his/her child are just as important as the training a medical professional completes. Together, if you listen to us and we listen to you we can provide the most comprehensive care for our child.

Please always remember, we cannot face each day with a gloom and doom attitude. We need to have hope and we need your support to raise our child to become everything that he/she can be, whatever that is!

Tips for Getting the Most Out of a Doctor's Visit

Cameron had so many doctor and therapy appointments his first year that through trial and error I found certain tips and tricks that worked well and that I continue to use whenever we have an appointment. Although the ideas are simple, they do work and sometimes when you are overwhelmed with so many visits this list may help to make your life a little easier. Here they are:

1. **List of Questions:** Each visit that I attend I bring with me a list of all questions that I have. On this paper I also list any referrals I need to request as well as prescription refills. I start my list of questions often weeks before a visit and just keep adding to it. I always keep these lists in my diaper bag in an area that I also keep all of Cam's referrals in.

2. **Bring someone with you:** I have found it very helpful to always have someone with me when I have an appointment for Cameron. Having an extra person is important because I am guaranteed to have someone to keep Cameron occupied while I ask the questions I have. I also find that I am able to listen to each answer with my fullest attention and ask any additional questions that then arise.

3. **Bring a special toy or book:** I always pack a special little toy or book in my bag to bring to an appointment. I find these surprises to really help after we are taken into an exam room but before the doctor comes in.

4. **Bring plenty of drinks and food:** Cameron's specialists are located thirty-five miles from our house and so I always make sure I pack plenty of sippy cups of his rice milk and a lot of little snacks. I find that I am totally prepared for times when we encounter delays due to medical emergencies or traffic.

5. **Have your paperwork prepared:** I always have my referral, insurance card, co-pay and any questionnaires that I have received for the appointment completed and in the front of my diaper bag so that I can quickly hand them to the receptionist when we check in.

6. **Referrals:** If your insurance requires that you have a referral to see specialists, like our insurance, you want to make sure that you give your child's primary care physician plenty of time to prepare it. Cam's pediatrician and I discussed what would be the best way to request referrals and we chose to have me fax the requests seven to ten days prior to appointment date. It has worked out great because I write down on my calendar when to send each fax and then I do not forget and when the referrals are ready I get a call and

pick them up. I also am able to request several different referrals at once without taking a nurse's time to explain over the phone what I need. As soon as I pick them up I put them in the diaper bag by the other referrals.

Resources that We Have Found Helpful as Parents of a Child with Special Needs

1. **Family**

   We have been blessed to have many family members who have provided support throughout Cameron's entire journey. They are the ones who call and e-mail us on a consistent basis, whether Cameron is in the hospital or home doing well. They are the people we can cry to and they will not quickly hang up the phone or change the subject. They listen and although they might not know exactly how we are feeling they do care and want to help us in any way they can. They are also the ones that we can share Cameron's accomplishments with and they celebrate just as enthusiastically as we do.

2. **Friends**

   We have learned through this journey who are true friends are. They are our friends through the good times and the hard times. When Cameron is struggling and we might not be able to join them for play dates they still invite us and continue to invite us. They call and again let us share our joys and fears. And never do they tell us not to feel a certain way or that they know exactly how we feel because they do not. They also offer to help in any way they can, be it having Abby over for a special play date, accompanying me to a doctor's appointment or going to the grocery store for us. Although we rarely need to accept their offers the fact that they do offer and are willing to help us makes all the difference.

3. **Parent Liaison from Early Intervention**

   When Cameron was just seven weeks old and we learned of his extensive brain damage, Cameron's pediatric neurologist referred us to our Early Intervention office to help arrange for evaluations of Cam to determine what therapeutic services that he would need and to coordinate payment of those services with our insurance company. In addition to providing that level of support, Early Intervention employs a parent liaison that helps support a family through the process of acceptance of having a child with special needs. The parent liaison is a parent of a child with special needs as well and further along in his/her journey into this new world of parenting. Our parent liaison, Angela, provided a listening ear when I cried with anger over Cameron getting sick, when I cried with worry about Cameron's future, when I shared each milestone with her, be it a small or a large milestone, when I shared the disappointment I felt in the people in our lives that for whatever reason were not and continue to not be our support people. She has walked through each step of this journey with us, not only because it was her job but because she is a caring person whose passion has become helping other parents to find the incredible joy that accompanies raising a child with special needs.

4. **The medical support staff**

    We have been blessed to have so many wonderful medical professionals who truly care not only for Cameron but also for our entire family. Each of the nurses and medical assistants that are part of Cameron's team are truly dedicated and committed to helping us. They have allowed us to cry as we have faced new obstacles and again to celebrate each accomplishment, regardless of its magnitude. They have taken extra time to make Abby feel special and a part of this process because she is one of the most influential people in Cameron's life and he is likewise in hers.

5. **Cameron's Specialists**

    Each specialist that Cameron sees has provided an enormous amount of knowledge to Tim and me. Knowledge certainly is a powerful tool in helping your child to become everything they can be. Each visit we have been encouraged to ask any and all questions we have. We have also been encouraged to ask a question repeatedly until we fully understand the answers. We have received calls during Cam's times of struggles. And we have been assured that the support we need as a family will always be there for us—and 4 ½ years into our journey I can assure you that this is the truth.

6. **Therapists**

    Cameron has worked with a physical therapist, occupational therapist, speech therapist and developmental therapist. Each has provided Cameron with the support he has needed to work hard to achieve his therapy goals. They have made the sessions fun to encourage Cameron to continue working hard rather than allow him to quit out of discouragement. They have open their hearts to getting to know Cameron and who he is and what his passions are (music!) and have never seen him for the disability that he has. And they have provided our family with the tools to also help Cameron at home and to incorporate the therapy goals into our everyday lives.

7. **School Personnel**

    Cameron's special education teacher, Miss Jeanie, has helped Cameron to find a love for learning in a safe and accepting environment. She has fostered a relationship of trust with Cameron that has resulted in Cameron asking her to bend "down on her knees" when he arrives daily so that he can give her a big hug. And she has shared with us that that is the best way to start her day! Cameron's one on one aide, Miss Carolyn, has provided Cameron with the encouragement to venture out in the classroom and interact with the other students rather than only the adults. She has set realistic and consistent expectations for what is acceptable and non-acceptable behavior and has made Cameron responsible for following these guidelines. And she has made him love the drive to school, knowing that he will greeted by an amazing woman who truly loves each and every moment she spends with him. Additionally, each therapist and support staff has enjoyed Cameron's bubbly and silly personality and have spent the time to encourage him to keep reaching to achieve more. Throughout the school year, as a family we have also been supported with the struggles and challenges Cam has faced in terms of impulse control issues. We have been provided with suggestions that might work at home and a shoulder to lean on during those rough patches. And each school member has acknowledged and supported the enormous role that Abby plays in Cameron's life and progress.

8. Parents of Children with Special Needs

We have been blessed to also have parents of children with special needs as our family friends as well. Some of which have children older than ours and some with younger children. We are able to share our thoughts and feelings in a supportive, nonjudgmental atmosphere. We gain support but also find so much strength in being able to help other parents as well. Some of the parents we have met through Cameron's special education program, others through Early Intervention, and then others through park district programs in our community.

www.cameronsjourney.com

Another resource that is now available and we hope you will visit often is Cameron's Web site, www.cameronsjourney.com. Although I authored this Web site, the Web site would not be in existence today without the generosity of both Michael and Jessica Knight. When I decided to start sharing Cameron's story I wanted to develop a Web site but did not have any technical expertise with Web site development. Jessica and I have known each other through cyber space for several years now through a parenting Web site we both belong to. When I posted a question on the board to ask advice on Web site development, Jessica immediately e-mailed me back and said that her husband, Michael, would be able to help. Michael has designed an amazing Web site that allows every visitor to read about Cameron's story, learn about our family, his medical team, media happenings as well as access a link to the video montage that I created of Cameron. As time has passed and Cameron's story has been featured in multiple newspapers and I have had many opportunities to present his story, Michael has helped to keep Cam's Web site up to date. We hope you will enjoy visiting the Web site and find the information useful. And thank you again Jessica and Michael, your creativity and generosity are appreciated.

Steven, Jessica, Michael and Bryce

Raising Awareness with www.infowindow.com

I wanted to find a unique way to raise awareness about Cameron's Journey and I decided to search the Internet to order a window cling with Cameron's Web site on it for my car. I had no idea that what I would find would be much more than a simple window cling with a Web site on it. I came across the Web site, www.infowindow.com, and e-mailed the owner, Jim, to see if he would be interested in helping us design a window mural for the back of my Honda CRV so that we could raise awareness about Cameron's Journey. Little did I know that what we would receive would be a very beautiful mural of some of my favorite pictures of Cam and our family that would make each and every person who sees it want to visit www.cameronsjourney.com to learn more about our family's journey. Here is a copy of the logo that Jim and his design team created. Thank you so much Jim for helping to raise awareness about the need to Never Say Never!

Contact Information for Becki Enck

If you are interested in contacting Becki Enck to schedule a presentation or media appearance, please e-mail her at info@cameronsjourney.com.

978-0-595-49005-9
0-595-49005-0

Lightning Source UK Ltd.
Milton Keynes UK
12 September 2009

143621UK00001B/186/P